Lady Killers: Beneath the Surface of Evil

Mahe Dee

Published by pinky, 2024.

LADY KILLERS: BENEATH THE SURFACE OF EVIL

First edition. October 7, 2024.

Copyright © 2024 Mahe Dee.

ISBN: 979-8227509895

Written by Mahe Dee.

Table of Contents

Preface

E vil, in its most chilling form, often lurks in the most unexpected places, beneath the surface of seemingly ordinary lives. The stories in this book are not just accounts of crime, but deep explorations into the darkest corners of the human psyche. Each tale is a haunting reminder that sometimes, the greatest horrors come not from the unknown but from those closest to us—parents, partners, and trusted loved ones. This book has been written to offer readers a glimpse into the true depths of human depravity, as well as the psychological complexities that drive people to commit unspeakable acts.

The true stories of notorious female criminals that fill these pages are a chilling collection of some of history's most terrifying cases. These women, who were at first glance unremarkable—wives, mothers, and community members—each harbored a darkness that would eventually manifest in the most horrific of ways. Their crimes, often committed within the sacred confines of family life, challenge our deepest-held beliefs about trust, love, and maternal instincts.

This book has been written to serve several purposes. First, it seeks to explore the true events and characters that shaped these horrifying crimes. By understanding the individuals involved, their backgrounds, their mental states, and the conflicts that consumed them, we can better grasp the layers of complexity that lie behind the actions of female serial killers. Often, these crimes are driven by deep psychological issues, compounded by societal pressures and personal traumas. This book delves into the mental turmoil experienced by these women and how it led them down a path of destruction.

Secondly, this book has been written to offer a broader reflection on human nature. What drives someone to commit murder? What psychological mechanisms are at play? And why do some people, who seem perfectly ordinary on the outside, harbor such violent tendencies within? Each chapter will force readers to question their assumptions about evil and the people who commit it. This is not a book of judgment but of exploration—exploring how a mix of circumstances, mental illness, and unchecked emotions can culminate in devastating actions.

The stories presented here—those of Myra Hindley, Waneta Hoyt, Nannie Doss, Vera Renczi, and others—are not just retellings of facts. They delve deeply into the lives and minds of the women behind the crimes, offering readers a rare glimpse into the psychological battles that raged within them. Through detailed descriptions of their early lives, relationships, mental struggles, and the moment when they crossed the line from ordinary life to heinous acts, readers will get an intimate look at the inner workings of these notorious criminals.

These women shared one tragic commonality: beneath their outward appearance of normalcy lay brokenness, whether due to deep-seated personal trauma, abusive upbringings, or untreated mental illnesses. This book does not seek to excuse their actions but to illuminate the dark paths they traveled and to better understand the reasons behind their behavior. Through each story, readers will explore the horrifying reality that, for many of these women, the facade of everyday life hid a festering darkness that eventually spilled out in violence and death.

Why should readers explore this darkness? Why should we take a closer look at the stories of these female criminals? It is because, within these tales, there are lessons to be learned—about human nature, society, mental illness, and the consequences of ignoring warning signs. These stories act as cautionary tales, warning us of the hidden dangers that can reside behind closed doors. They show us the importance of vigilance, empathy, and early intervention in situations of psychological distress. More than anything, they remind us that evil is not always an abstract concept but something that can manifest in the most unexpected ways.

The women in this book each had their own motives—be it greed, jealousy, possessiveness, or the desperate need to control those around them. Yet, they all shared the ability to deceive those closest to them. They wore masks of normalcy, blending into their communities, and in many cases, winning the trust and sympathy of their neighbors, friends, and even families. The subtlety with which they concealed their true intentions makes their stories all the more chilling. This book brings to light the ease with which these women manipulated those around them, making their eventual betrayal even more devastating.

Readers should approach this book with a mixture of curiosity and caution. The stories within are not easy to read; they deal with the most sensitive and painful aspects of human existence—betrayal, death, and the destruction of familial bonds. Yet, they are important stories to tell. Through these accounts, we gain insights not just into the criminal mind but into the vulnerabilities of society and the shortcomings of the systems designed to protect us. Many of these crimes could have been prevented had there been earlier recognition of the signs of psychological distress and intervention.

Finally, this book serves as a reminder of the resilience of human nature. Though these stories are about loss and destruction, they also show the strength of those who survived, the determination of law enforcement to uncover the truth, and the changes in the legal and healthcare systems that came about as a result of these tragic events. These stories, though dark, offer hope that through awareness and understanding, we can better protect those who are vulnerable and prevent future tragedies from occurring.

In reading Lady Killers: Beneath the Surface of Evil, you are invited into a world of hidden horrors, where outward appearances often conceal the darkest intentions. Through these stories, you will confront the uncomfortable reality that even the most familiar and trusted individuals can harbor dangerous secrets. You will delve into the psyches of some of history's most notorious female criminals and explore the circumstances that led to their shocking actions. This book does not offer simple answers but invites you to question, reflect, and better understand the complexities of human behavior. Prepare yourself for a journey through the most unsettling corners of the human mind—where evil often lies just beneath the surface.

—**Author**

1. A Dark Descent

Aileen Wuornos sat in the dim room, her eyes darting to the window, the walls closing in around her. Born into chaos, she had been searching for peace all her life, yet peace eluded her. The world had been cruel, and so had she. The air in the room was thick with the smell of cigarettes and the weight of her past. Her memories were relentless, playing in her mind like an endless, haunting reel of film.

Aileen came into the world on February 29, 1956, in Rochester, Michigan. Her parents, Diane and Leo, were a storm of dysfunction. Leo was a diagnosed schizophrenic, locked up for sex crimes against children. He wasn't there when Aileen was born—he never would be, taking his own life in prison not long after. Diane, overwhelmed and unable to care for Aileen and her brother Keith, left them with their grandparents when Aileen was just four years old. It was a household of shadows and violence. Lauri Wuornos, her grandfather, was an alcoholic, who could shift from cold indifference to vicious rage in a heartbeat. Her grandmother, Britta, was distant and sickly, too weak to intervene in the nightmare that unfolded in their home.

Aileen, a small child with wide, untrusting eyes, learned to fend for herself in that house. By the time she was eleven, she had already been pulled into the cycle of abuse. Her mental state, fragile as it was, began to fracture. The world outside was no kinder. Boys at school didn't see her as a peer but as something to use. Aileen traded sexual favors for food, cigarettes, whatever she could get. It wasn't survival anymore—it was desperation. She was lost.

At fourteen, Aileen was expelled from her home after getting pregnant, allegedly from a rape by one of her grandfather's friends. She gave birth to a boy in 1971, but the child was quickly taken away and put up for adoption. It was the last flicker of innocence in Aileen's life before darkness consumed her completely. Homeless, and abandoned, she turned to prostitution to survive. Aileen roamed the streets like a ghost, slipping further from herself each day.

The years passed, and the world around Aileen blurred. She drank heavily, her nights spent in smoky biker bars where the only things sharper than the knives on men's belts were their words. Violence became her language. She never found stability, not even in relationships. Her brief marriage in 1976 to Lewis Gratz Fell, a wealthy yacht club president, ended after nine weeks—another car crash in the wreck of her life. The only person she ever truly connected with was Tyria Moore, a woman she met in 1986. Their love was one of the few constants in her chaotic life, but even that love couldn't save Aileen from herself.

The murders started in late 1989. Her first victim, Richard Mallory, was a convicted rapist. Aileen claimed she killed him in self-defense, and that he had tried to rape her. She pulled the trigger, felt the recoil, and heard the dull thud of his body hit the ground. She stared down at him, her heart pounding, but there was no regret in her eyes. At that moment, something inside her snapped. From there, it was like a dam had burst. Six more men would meet the same fate over the next year—David Spears, Charles Carskaddon, Troy Burress, Charles Humphreys, Peter Siems, and Walter Antonio. Each time she pulled the trigger, she told herself it was survival. But the truth was darker. It was anger. It was revenge against a world that had treated her with such cruelty.

Each man she killed seemed to bring her closer to the edge, but Aileen remained elusive, moving from one roadside to the next, hitchhiking, selling her body, and slipping through the cracks of a society that didn't care to look for her. But the walls were closing in. The faces of her victims haunted her dreams, though she tried to drown them with alcohol, with noise, with anything that could mute the screams in her head.

In January 1991, it all came crashing down. She was arrested in a bar, her face hardened, but behind the toughness, fear flickered in her eyes. Tyria, the woman she loved, the only person she had ever trusted, betrayed her. Tyria had been scared—she hadn't known about the murders at first, but once she did, the weight of Aileen's actions was too much to carry. Tyria cooperated with the police, and it was her testimony that would seal Aileen's fate.

The trial was a spectacle. Reporters buzzed around like vultures, feeding on every sordid detail of her life. The prosecution painted Aileen as a cold-blooded killer, but her defense tried to tell a different story—one of a woman scarred by trauma, shaped by abuse, desperate to survive. Aileen sat there, her expression blank, but her mind raced. She listened to people talk about her like she was an animal like she had never been a child, like she had never felt fear, pain, or love. The courtroom was suffocating, the weight of her actions crushing her.

In 1992, Aileen was sentenced to death. The public had little sympathy for her. Aileen Wuornos wasn't the victim anymore—she was the monster. But inside, she was still that broken little girl, lost in a world that had never cared for her. The years dragged on as she awaited execution, her mental state deteriorating further. Her once fiery spirit was dulled by the weight of her own anger and bitterness.

In her final interview before her execution in 2002, Aileen's voice cracked with rage and sorrow. "I am sorry for everything I've done," she said, her eyes dark and hollow, "I'll be up in heaven while y'all are rotting in hell." The words cut through the air, leaving a bitter taste. They weren't just meant for the men she killed—they were meant for everyone who had hurt her, who had failed her.

On October 9, 2002, Aileen Wuornos was executed by lethal injection. As the drugs coursed through her veins, her body stilled. But the questions surrounding her life, her crimes, and her legacy remained. Was she a victim of her circumstances? Or was she simply a violent killer?

Her story, full of pain, anger, and tragedy, would be told and retold in books, documentaries, and films. The world would never forget Aileen Wuornos, but the world would never truly understand her either. She had lived a life of survival, but it was a life devoid of hope, a life that had never been allowed to flourish.

In the end, Aileen's life wasn't about justice or redemption. It was about a system that had failed her from the start. She died, not as a monster, but as a product of the darkness that had shaped her. Her name remains infamous, a grim reminder of the violence that can arise from the ashes of broken lives.

2. The Baby Butcher

The cold air of Victorian England wrapped itself around the bustling streets, hiding the darker secrets beneath the surface. Amidst the fog and grime of the 19th century, Amelia Dyer moved like a shadow, blending in with the crowd, a woman whose face betrayed no guilt. Her story wasn't one of fleeting tragedy—it was one of calculated evil, where greed and deception paved the way to the most horrific crimes. She would come to be known as the "Baby Butcher," and her actions would leave an indelible scar on the history of child welfare in England.

Born Amelia Elizabeth Hobley in 1837, in the small village of Pyle Marsh, near Bristol, England, she was the youngest of five children in a relatively well-off family. Her father, Samuel Hobley, was a shoemaker—a man who cared more about his business than his children, especially his youngest daughter. Her mother, Sarah, on the other hand, was a woman who became a stranger to herself. Typhus ravaged Sarah's body, and worse, her mind. Amelia watched her mother's violent fits, her terrifying hallucinations. The small girl, barely ten, would hold her breath, hoping her mother wouldn't notice her, wouldn't turn those wild eyes in her direction. Caring for her mentally unstable mother left deep scars on Amelia's mind, scars that would never heal.

When Sarah finally died in 1848, Amelia must have felt some twisted relief, but any chance of peace was short-lived. The gloom of the Hobley household lingered even in her absence. Amelia, a bright and curious child, had developed a love for reading and writing, but these joys were soon snatched away. After her mother's death, she was sent to live with an aunt in Bristol, training as a nurse. This skill would serve her well, but not in the way anyone expected. What should have been a path of care and healing became a road toward darkness.

In 1861, Amelia married George Thomas, a man old enough to be her father. George was 59; Amelia lied about her age, claiming to be 30, though she was barely 24. George reduced his age too, for the sake of appearances. Their life together was far from idyllic. George was frail, and Amelia, though a new mother to their daughter Ellen, was restless. She was not content with the life of a nurse or a caregiver. She wanted more—money, security, and a way out of the poverty that always seemed to creep around the edges of their lives. When George died in 1869, Amelia was left alone, widowed, and desperate.

The baby farming business was a common practice in Victorian England, where unwanted or illegitimate infants were given to women like Amelia, who promised to care for them in exchange for payment. Mothers, often shamed by society for having children out of wedlock, were eager to find a place for their babies, and Amelia took full advantage. At first, her baby farming seemed legitimate. She took in infants, promising to find them new homes. But soon, the façade cracked. The money she received from desperate mothers was never enough. She realized that it was more profitable to dispose of the babies rather than care for them.

Amelia's descent into murder began with opium. She would drug the infants, administering laudanum or "Mother's Friend" to keep them quiet. It was a common practice among baby farmers, but Amelia pushed it further. The babies often died from overdoses, their small bodies unable to handle the powerful drug. At first, these deaths seemed accidental—after all, infant mortality was high in Victorian England. But soon, Amelia abandoned any pretense of care. She stopped using drugs and began strangling the babies with white tape, a method that became her signature. She would wrap the tiny bodies in cloth and dump them in the river, erasing their short lives without a second thought.

Amelia's business grew. She changed her name and address frequently, evading detection as she moved through different towns. Her clients, desperate single mothers, were too ashamed or too poor to ask questions. They handed over their babies and the little money they had, hoping for a miracle. Amelia gave them lies instead.

The murders continued for years, but in 1896, her luck ran out. The body of a baby girl, Helena Fry, was pulled from the River Thames, wrapped in material traced back to Amelia. Her calm exterior began to crack. Investigators soon uncovered a gruesome trail, linking Amelia to the deaths of multiple infants. Her arrest sent shockwaves through Victorian society.

The trial was swift and brutal, just like Amelia's crimes. In court, she showed little emotion. Witnesses described her as cold, manipulative, a woman driven by greed. "I have nothing to say," were her final words to the court when given a chance to defend herself. The press and public alike were horrified by the revelations. Amelia Dyer wasn't just a murderer—she was a monster who had preyed on the most vulnerable. Her face was splashed across newspapers, and her name whispered in fear.

On June 10, 1896, Amelia Dyer was hanged for her crimes. She showed no remorse, no sorrow for the lives she had taken. In her mind, the babies were nothing more than a means to an end, tools in her pursuit of wealth. Her execution brought an end to her reign of terror, but her story left a dark stain on England's history.

Amelia Dyer's crimes weren't just a result of her greed; they were the product of a broken system. The baby farming industry flourished in the shadows, where society's unwanted children were forgotten. Amelia exploited this system, using it to hide her murders for years. Her case forced the public to confront the horrors of baby farming, leading to reforms in child protection laws. The Infant Life Protection Act of 1897 was passed in response to her crimes, ensuring stricter regulations on the care of foster children.

But no law could undo the damage she had done. Amelia Dyer's name became synonymous with cruelty, her story a chilling reminder of the darkness that can fester in the cracks of society. Even today, her legacy lingers as one of the most infamous killers in British history—a woman who, driven by greed, had become the face of pure evil.

Her final words, "I have nothing to say," still echo, a stark reflection of the emptiness inside her. She took her secrets to the grave, but the truth of her actions would never be buried. Amelia Dyer may be gone, but her story remains a grim warning of what can happen when society turns a blind eye to its most vulnerable members. The babies she killed will never be forgotten, their short lives a testament to the horrors she wrought.

3. A Deceptive Nurse's Dark Deeds

In the quiet streets of Finchley, London, a small maternity home stood with an air of respectability. Its owner, Amelia Sach, was known as a calm, collected nurse who offered a compassionate service to unmarried women, providing care for their unwanted babies and promising them a better future. But behind the kind face and gentle words, there lurked a darkness that would shock the nation. Amelia Sach's crimes weren't those of passion or anger but of cold calculation, driven by greed and a complete lack of empathy. Alongside her accomplice, Annie Walters, she would become one of the most notorious baby killers in British history.

Amelia was born in 1867 in the rural village of Hampreston, Dorset, to George and Mary Anne Sach. Life in the Sach household was hard. Her parents were agricultural laborers, scraping by to feed their large family. Poverty was a constant shadow over Amelia's childhood, shaping her ambitions early on. The rural setting, and the struggle for food and survival, left deep marks on young Amelia. She grew up watching her parents toil, never quite breaking free of the cycle of hardship. As she matured, she realized that she didn't want to live like that—she wanted more, much more.

Amelia left school early to help support her family, working in various domestic roles. She learned the art of care, picking up skills that would later serve her well in her career as a nurse. Yet, Amelia was no ordinary caregiver. While she learned to soothe the sick and aid the vulnerable, her mind harbored a growing hunger for financial stability and success.

In 1896, Amelia married William Horace Henry Stiles, a builder. They moved to Finchley, hoping to start fresh. But marriage didn't bring her the life she had dreamed of. Financial strain plagued them, and the couple remained childless—a fact that seemed to fuel Amelia's growing resentment. She watched as other families built their futures, raising children and prospering, while her own life remained empty of the things she craved. Her husband worked hard, but it was never enough. She needed more, and in her desperation, she found her opportunity in the shadows of society.

At the turn of the 20th century, the baby farming industry was a little-known but widespread practice. Unwed mothers, often shunned by society, paid women like Amelia to care for their babies, with the promise that the infants would be adopted into loving homes. The reality was often much darker. Amelia, seeing the opportunity, opened a maternity home in Finchley, where she promised desperate mothers that their babies would be taken care of. Her clients, vulnerable and filled with guilt, handed over their infants and the little money they had, believing they were giving their children a better life.

But Amelia had no intention of caring for those babies. She soon partnered with Annie Walters, a former midwife with a history of drug addiction and questionable morals. Together, the two women devised a plan that would bring them quick, easy money—without the burden of actually raising the children. Instead of finding homes for the infants, they simply killed them.

Amelia was methodical. The babies were brought to her home, where they were given a fatal dose of chlorodyne, a widely available sedative that was deadly in the wrong amounts. The drug would lull the infants into permanent sleep, their fragile bodies unable to handle the overdose. Afterward, Amelia and Annie would dress the babies in new clothes—an eerie act of final care—before disposing of their bodies, either in the river or buried in shallow graves. It was a horrific business, made worse by the cold efficiency with which they operated. To the outside world, Amelia remained the caring nurse, a woman to be trusted with the lives of newborns. She kept up appearances with ease, blending into the community while secretly profiting off the deaths of innocent children.

The operation might have continued unnoticed for much longer had it not been for one mistake. In 1902, the body of an infant was found in a nearby river, and the investigation led back to Amelia Sach's maternity home. The authorities began to unravel the horror behind her respectable façade. Evidence of multiple infant deaths surfaced, and Amelia's long-held secret was exposed. Panic and outrage swept through the community as the extent of her crimes became known.

Amelia Sach and Annie Walters were arrested, and the trial that followed was one of the most scandalous in British criminal history. The court was filled with mothers who had trusted their children to Amelia, their faces lined with grief and disbelief. How could the kind nurse who had offered them comfort be responsible for such monstrous acts? Amelia sat in the dock, her face pale and emotionless, as the prosecution detailed the murders of the infants. She showed little remorse, maintaining her innocence with icy calmness.

"I am innocent of any crime," Amelia declared during her trial, her voice unwavering. But the evidence was overwhelming. Annie Walters, her partner in crime, was less composed. She broke down in court, her addiction-ravaged face twitching as she pointed the finger at Amelia, hoping to save herself by shifting the blame. The partnership that had once seemed so strong crumbled under the weight of their guilt.

In 1903, both women were found guilty of murder and sentenced to death. On the morning of February 3, 1903, Amelia Sach and Annie Walters were hanged for their crimes. Amelia's final moments were marked by a stoic silence. She went to the gallows with the same coldness that had defined her life. Her final words, "I am innocent," echoed in the minds of those who had followed the case, but few believed her. The nation breathed a sigh of relief as one of its most infamous criminals was finally gone.

Amelia Sach's story didn't end with her death. The public outrage sparked by her crimes led to significant changes in child protection laws. The Infant Life Protection Act of 1908 was introduced to prevent the exploitation of vulnerable children, providing stricter regulations for the care of fostered and adopted infants. While Amelia herself never contributed to any positive change, her horrific actions forced society to confront the dark reality of baby farming and to take steps to protect those who could not protect themselves.

Today, Amelia Sach is remembered as one of the most notorious figures in British criminal history, her name synonymous with betrayal and cruelty. Her life serves as a chilling reminder of what can happen when greed and exploitation go unchecked. She used her skills as a nurse, not to heal, but to destroy. And while the reforms that followed her crimes helped to save countless children, the innocent lives lost to her murderous scheme will never be forgotten.

Amelia Sach, the seemingly respectable nurse from Finchley, had deceived everyone around her. But in the end, justice caught up with her. Her legacy, one of horror and revulsion, lingers as a powerful reminder of the darkness that can hide behind the most innocent of faces.

4. The Poisoner's Betrayal

Anna Maria Zwanziger stood by the kitchen window, her hands working methodically as she prepared the evening's meal. The smell of herbs mingled with something far more dangerous—arsenic, her weapon of choice. She was calm and deliberate, her face betraying none of the darkness lurking within. Her employers trusted her, and that trust would be their undoing. For years, Zwanziger had quietly positioned herself as a domestic servant, offering care, loyalty, and efficiency, all while hiding a deadly secret. She wasn't just managing households; she was plotting deaths, one spoonful at a time.

Born in 1760 in Nuremberg, Germany, Anna Maria Schönleben, as she was known before marriage, grew up in a modest household. Her father was a craftsman, and her mother managed their small home. Life wasn't easy for the family, and Anna's childhood was marked by financial struggles and emotional neglect. Her parents were distant, focused on survival, and there was little warmth in the Schönleben household. Anna learned early on that the world was a hard, unforgiving place, and in her formative years, she developed an obsession with control and power—things she felt she never had.

As a young woman, Anna received only a basic education, typical of her social class. She learned the domestic skills expected of her, cooking and cleaning, but there was little else to offer her any chance at a better life. When she married a man named Zwanziger in her early twenties, she believed it was her escape from poverty. But her marriage brought no happiness. Instead, it was a union filled with hardship and tension. They had several children, but the pressures of raising a family in poverty, combined with Anna's increasingly erratic behavior, made life unbearable. Eventually, her husband left her, abandoning Anna and their children to fend for themselves. The abandonment left her with deep resentment and an overwhelming desire for control.

Without a husband, and with children to feed, Anna turned to domestic work, a common profession for women in her position. She found employment as a housekeeper, moving from one wealthy household to another, relying on her reputation as a diligent worker. But behind her façade of reliability, Anna was desperate. Her heart was filled with bitterness, and her need for financial security took on a dangerous edge. She no longer saw her employers as people.

To her, they were obstacles, ones she would overcome in the most sinister way possible.

Anna's descent into murder began quietly. In her role as housekeeper, she was in charge of preparing food and medicine, and it was through these daily tasks that she found her opportunity. Her first known victim was her employer's wife. The woman had been ill for some time, and when Anna added arsenic to her food, the death seemed natural, even expected. No one suspected the quiet housekeeper, who had been so attentive and caring. And so, Anna got away with it. The sense of power she felt over life and death was intoxicating, and it wasn't long before she was poisoned again.

Arsenic was her chosen method. It was easy to obtain in small quantities, and it could be slipped into food or drink without anyone noticing. The poison worked slowly, causing her victims to suffer, their bodies wasting away as if from a natural illness. Anna took no joy in the suffering, but she didn't shy away from it either. In fact, she justified her actions to herself. She wasn't killing out of malice, she convinced herself, but to better her own life. These were merely sacrifices in her pursuit of survival. Her ability to distance herself emotionally from her victims allowed her to continue her deadly spree without guilt.

Anna moved from one household to the next, ingratiating herself with her employers while quietly plotting their deaths. She managed to avoid detection for several years, using her position of trust to shield her from suspicion. She was known as a hardworking, reliable housekeeper, and no one would have guessed that she harbored such dark intentions. Her employers respected her; they never saw the danger until it was too late.

But Anna's success couldn't last forever. One of her victims began to suspect something was wrong. After falling mysteriously ill, he noticed that his symptoms worsened after meals prepared by Anna. Distrust crept in, and eventually, he alerted the authorities. An investigation was launched, and it wasn't long before a pattern of deaths began to emerge, all linked to households where Anna had worked.

In 1809, Zwanziger was arrested. The investigation into her crimes revealed the true extent of her cruelty. She had poisoned not just her employers but also their family members and even fellow servants, anyone who stood in her way or posed a threat to her stability. The authorities were horrified by her lack of remorse. During her trial, Anna showed no sign of guilt. In fact, she justified her actions by saying, "I have not poisoned anyone out of hatred, but to better my condition." To her, these murders weren't crimes—they were simply necessary steps in her fight for survival.

The trial was widely covered in the press, and Anna Maria Zwanziger became a symbol of betrayal and cruelty. The public couldn't comprehend how a woman who had been trusted to care for others could turn so cold and calculating. But Anna had always been good at hiding her true self. Her outward appearance, that of a loyal servant, had masked the darkness within for years.

In the end, justice caught up with Anna Maria Zwanziger. She was convicted of multiple murders and sentenced to death. In 1811, she was executed by beheading, her life ending as coldly as she had lived it. As the executioner's axe fell, her final words echoed in the minds of those who had followed her case: "I have not poisoned anyone out of hatred." But the truth was far darker—Anna's life had been driven by greed, control, and an insatiable need for power over others.

Anna's story didn't just end with her death. Her crimes sent shockwaves through society, forcing a reckoning with the trust placed in domestic workers. Her case led to increased scrutiny of household employment practices and sparked changes in the way employers monitored their servants. The quiet poisonings of Anna Zwanziger had exposed a terrifying vulnerability—one that the public could no longer ignore.

Today, Anna Maria Zwanziger is remembered as one of Germany's most infamous poisoners. Her story, one of manipulation, greed, and betrayal, serves as a chilling reminder of the dangers lurking behind a mask of loyalty and trust. What made her truly terrifying wasn't just the number of her victims but the calculated, methodical way in which she exploited the vulnerability of those who trusted her. Her ability to deceive, to remain undetected for so long, cemented her place in history as one of the most cold-blooded killers of her time.

Anna Maria Zwanziger's life was a tragedy of her own making. She had been born into hardship, but instead of seeking a way out through honest means, she chose a path of destruction. Her legacy is one of horror, a reminder of the capacity for evil that can reside in even the most ordinary of people. Her name will forever be associated with betrayal, cruelty, and the dark potential of unchecked greed.

5. The Mistress of Death

B elle Gunness was not a woman one would easily forget. Standing tall and strong, she commanded attention wherever she went, her presence filling the room with an unsettling air. Few could have imagined that beneath her seemingly respectable façade lay the heart of a cold-blooded killer, a woman driven by greed, cruelty, and an insatiable desire for control. Born as Brynhild Paulsdatter Storset on November 11, 1859, in the bleak and unforgiving landscape of Selbu, Norway, Belle's early life was shaped by hardship, poverty, and deprivation. It was a childhood that would forge her into one of history's most notorious female serial killers.

Belle's upbringing in Norway was nothing short of bleak. Her father, Paul Pedersen Storset, was a stonemason, a man who worked tirelessly but struggled to provide for his family. Her mother, Berit Olsdatter, managed the household, but with several children and scarce resources, life was a constant battle. The family lived in a small, cold house, typical of rural Norway, where winters were long and unforgiving. Belle grew up knowing only struggle and scarcity, and from a young age, she harbored a deep resentment for her circumstances. She was determined to escape the poverty that had defined her early years, and this resolve would shape her ruthless actions later in life.

In 1881, seeking a better life, Belle emigrated to the United States, leaving behind her family and the cold winds of Norway. She settled in Chicago, where she married Mads Ditlev Anton Sorenson three years later. The couple seemed to build a quiet life together, but even in this new chapter, Belle's hunger for wealth and security simmered beneath the surface. They had four children, but two died under mysterious circumstances—deaths that later raised suspicion. When Mads himself died in 1900, reportedly from heart failure, whispers of foul play began to circulate. Belle, however, had anticipated this moment well. She collected on his life insurance, walking away with a tidy sum, and used the money to buy a farm in La Porte, Indiana. It was here, in the quiet isolation of the countryside, that Belle Gunness would fully reveal the monster she had become.

The farm at La Porte became a graveyard of secrets. Isolated from prying eyes, Belle began placing personal ads in newspapers, targeting wealthy men with promises of marriage and a prosperous future. She lured suitors from across the country, all eager to meet the charming and supposedly successful widow. "Come to my farm," her letters would read, "and let us build a life together." The men arrived, expecting a new beginning, but what they found was death. One by one, they disappeared, leaving behind no trace but the money and valuables they had brought with them.

Belle was clever, and meticulous in her planning. She killed these men with cold precision, using various methods—sometimes poison, sometimes blunt force. Afterward, she dismembered their bodies and buried them in shallow graves on her farm. Her victims became just another part of the soil, their identities erased, their futures stolen. The neighbors were none the wiser. Belle maintained her facade of respectability, appearing to be a hardworking, kind woman who was merely unlucky in love. Her children played in the yard, her farm thrived, and no one questioned the steady stream of men who came and never left.

Her crimes might have continued undetected for years, but in 1908, the unthinkable happened. A fire consumed Belle's farmhouse, reducing it to smoldering ruins. In the aftermath, authorities found the charred remains of several bodies, including those of Belle's children. Among the bodies was the decapitated corpse of a woman, initially believed to be Belle herself. However, the discovery of multiple other bodies buried on the property soon raised questions. The authorities began to dig, and what they uncovered shocked the nation.

Buried in the farm's soil were the remains of countless men, each one lured to their deaths by Belle's cunning promises. As investigators pieced together the gruesome evidence, it became clear that Belle had been running a deadly scheme for years. She had used personal ads to prey on the vulnerable, exploiting their hopes for love and companionship. But where was Belle? The decapitated body found in the fire was never definitively identified as hers. Some believed she had faked her death, disappearing into the night to start anew somewhere else, leaving chaos and death in her wake. Others speculated that she had been murdered by one of her victims, finally meeting the same fate she had inflicted on so many. The truth, however, was never confirmed, and Belle's ultimate fate remains a mystery to this day.

Throughout the investigation, one thing became clear: Belle Gunness had been driven by an insatiable greed, a hunger for wealth that knew no bounds. Each murder had been calculated, a cold and deliberate step in her pursuit of financial gain. She was methodical in her approach, never leaving behind evidence that could point directly to her. In the quiet isolation of her farm, she had wielded life and death with terrifying ease, showing no empathy for the lives she destroyed.

Belle's ability to deceive those around her was perhaps her most chilling trait. Neighbors and acquaintances described her as "a woman of unusual strength and intelligence," someone who could charm and manipulate with ease. She presented herself as a hardworking, respectable member of the community, a widow simply trying to raise her children. In reality, she was a predator, lurking behind a mask of normalcy, ready to strike at any moment. Her calm demeanor, and her ability to hide her true nature, made her all the more dangerous.

The discovery of Belle's crimes sent shockwaves through society. Her case exposed the darker side of personal ads and the vulnerability of those who sought companionship through them. The public outcry that followed led to increased scrutiny of such ads and the introduction of measures to protect individuals from exploitation. But no law could undo the horror Belle had unleashed. Her name became synonymous with betrayal and cruelty, her story a chilling reminder of the dangers lurking behind seemingly innocent facades.

Belle Gunness's legacy is one of horror, a tale of manipulation, greed, and murder that continues to fascinate and terrify. Her ability to evade detection for so long, to charm her victims and then ruthlessly dispose of them, cemented her place in history as one of the most notorious female serial killers of all time. To this day, her story raises questions about the capacity for evil, the darkness that can reside within the human heart.

The "Hell's Belle" had claimed the lives of many, but in the end, her own fate remains shrouded in mystery. Did she perish in the fire, or did she escape to continue her deadly game elsewhere? The answer may never be known, but one thing is certain: Belle Gunness left behind a trail of blood and death, her actions a grim reminder of the lengths some will go to in pursuit of power and wealth.

6. The Kind-Hearted Killer

B ertha Gifford walked quietly through the fields of rural Missouri, her soft footsteps crunching on the leaves beneath her feet. The peaceful countryside was her home, a place where she was known and loved. Born as Bertha Alice Williams on October 30, 1872, she had grown up surrounded by the gentle hum of farm life, the warm summers and crisp winters shaping her childhood. The community in Morse Mill saw her as kind, compassionate, and always willing to lend a hand when sickness struck. But beneath that warmth, something far more sinister was taking root.

Bertha's early life seemed idyllic from the outside. Her parents, William Poindexter Williams and Matilda Williams, were hard-working farmers. Their life was modest, but they provided for their children as best they could. The summers were filled with the sounds of crickets and birds, and Bertha often played in the dense woods with her siblings. The winters brought silence and stillness, but they also taught Bertha about survival. Life on the farm was simple, but it was hard work, and from an early age, she learned to be strong and capable.

At school, Bertha was quiet, diligent, and focused. Her education was basic—just enough to read, write, and do arithmetic. In many ways, she seemed like any other farm girl of her time, but as she grew older, her interest in medicine began to bloom. Her mother, Matilda, taught her about herbal remedies and natural cures, which sparked something deep within her. Bertha took to nursing the sick, learning how to ease pain and bring comfort to the ailing.

In 1894, Bertha married Henry Graham, and together they had a daughter, Lila. Bertha's life seemed to take on the shape of a typical American farm wife. But tragedy struck when Henry died unexpectedly, leaving her widowed with a young child. Grief and uncertainty gripped her, but Bertha pressed on, determined to make a life for herself and Lila. She married Eugene Gifford, a local farmer, in 1907, and they had a son named James. The Gifford family moved to Catawissa, Missouri, where Bertha became known for her tireless efforts as a nurse, always ready to care for those in need. But dark whispers were beginning to circulate.

Bertha's nursing skills were widely praised. She had an almost magical ability to bring comfort to the sick, often cooking meals and preparing homemade remedies for her patients. Her reputation as a kind, selfless woman spread, and she was the first person called when someone fell ill. But as time passed, some of her patients didn't recover. They died, often quietly, in their beds, with Bertha by their side.

At first, no one suspected a thing. In those days, death was an accepted part of life, and it wasn't uncommon for people to pass away from illness. Bertha would console the grieving families, offering her prayers and sympathy. Yet, as the deaths began to mount, a pattern started to emerge. Her patients weren't just dying—they were being poisoned.

Bertha had become adept at using arsenic and other poisons, slipping them into the food and medicine of those she was supposed to be helping. Her victims, some of whom were members of her own family, suffered slow and painful deaths, unaware that the very woman they trusted with their lives was ending them. The community remained blissfully unaware, believing her to be a saintly figure, dedicated to their well-being. They had no reason to doubt her—after all, who would suspect a caring nurse of murder?

For nearly two decades, Bertha's crimes went unnoticed. She maintained her facade of innocence, all while secretly taking the lives of at least 17 people. Her motives were unclear—was it for financial gain, a twisted desire for control, or some dark compulsion? No one could say for sure. But what was certain was her ability to manipulate those around her, using her position of trust to hide her true nature.

In 1928, Bertha's luck ran out. Suspicion had been quietly growing in the community, and when one of her victims' families pushed for an investigation, the truth began to unravel. Authorities exhumed the bodies of several of her patients, and the results were damning. Traces of arsenic were found in the bodies, linking Bertha to their deaths. The kind-hearted nurse was now a suspect in a string of murders that shocked the rural Missouri community to its core.

Bertha was arrested, and her trial became a sensational event. Neighbors and friends, who had once trusted her with their lives, were horrified. "She was always so kind," one neighbor said in disbelief. "It's hard to believe she could do something so horrible." But the evidence was undeniable. Bertha had poisoned those who relied on her, betraying their trust in the most horrific way imaginable.

Throughout the trial, Bertha maintained her innocence. She claimed she had never harmed anyone and that the deaths were simply unfortunate coincidences. But the jury didn't believe her. She was found guilty of two murders, though it was widely suspected that the true number of her victims was much higher. Due to her deteriorating mental state, she was declared insane and sent to a mental institution, where she would live out the rest of her days.

Bertha's story left a deep scar on the community. The people of Catawissa and Morse Mill, who had once viewed her as a beloved nurse and caregiver, were forced to grapple with the fact that one of their own had committed unspeakable acts. The case also had wider implications, leading to increased awareness of poisoning as a method of murder and prompting changes in forensic practices. It became clear that even those who seemed trustworthy could harbor dark secrets.

Bertha Gifford's legacy is one of duality. On the surface, she was a devoted wife, mother, and nurse—a woman who brought comfort and care to those in need. But beneath that exterior was a heart capable of unimaginable cruelty. Her ability to present herself as a saintly figure while secretly committing heinous crimes makes her one of the most chilling figures in early 20th-century criminal history.

Today, Bertha Gifford is remembered as one of America's earliest female serial killers. Her story serves as a grim reminder that appearances can be deceiving and that evil can lurk in even the most ordinary of places. She manipulated her way into the lives of her victims, using their trust as a weapon. Her actions continue to fascinate and horrify those who study criminal behavior, offering a dark glimpse into the complexities of human nature.

In the end, Bertha Gifford's life was a tragic tale of dual identities—one of a caring nurse and the other of a cold-blooded killer. The small towns she once called home would never forget the horrors she brought into their midst, nor the lives she extinguished in her twisted pursuit of control.

7. The Angel of Death

B everley Allitt's life began in the quiet, close-knit community of Grantham, Lincolnshire. Born on October 4, 1968, to Richard and Lillian Allitt, she grew up in a modest household with three siblings. Life in the English countryside was slow and predictable—foggy mornings, cool winters, and mild summers that left the fields green but damp. There was nothing remarkable about Beverley's early years on the surface. Yet, beneath the normality of her childhood, something darker stirred.

From a young age, Beverley had an insatiable need for attention. She frequently feigned illness, often visiting doctors for minor or self-inflicted injuries. This fascination with illness became a defining feature of her personality. Beverley's quiet demeanor at school masked a deep-seated loneliness. She was a solitary figure, preferring to be alone, and never fitting in with her peers. She developed an obsession with the medical world, fascinated by hospitals, nurses, and the power they wielded over life and death.

Her parents, Richard and Lillian, worked hard to provide for their children. Richard, a council worker, and Lillian, a school cleaner, instilled in their children the importance of responsibility and care for others. But Beverley felt overshadowed by her siblings, often competing for her parents' attention. Her craving for recognition and validation only deepened as she grew older, and it found its outlet in her interest in nursing.

In her early twenties, Beverley enrolled in nursing school, but her journey to becoming a nurse was anything but smooth. She struggled academically, failing her nursing exams multiple times. Despite her failures, Beverley was relentless in her pursuit of becoming a nurse. Her persistence finally paid off when she secured a position as a State Enrolled Nurse at Grantham and Kesteven Hospital. It was a small victory for her—a role that placed her in a position of care and authority, something she had long desired.

It was here, in the hospital's children's ward, that Beverley found herself surrounded by vulnerable patients—children whose lives were in her hands. The trust placed in her by parents, colleagues, and the system became the foundation for her sinister actions. Beneath her calm, caring exterior, she was ready to exploit that trust for her twisted need for attention and control.

23

Beverley could manipulate those around her, and in the children's ward, she had the perfect opportunity.

Over 59 days in 1991, Beverley Allitt unleashed a reign of terror that would leave the nation in shock. She began administering lethal doses of insulin and other substances to her young patients. Some survived the attacks, but many did not. Four children—Liam Taylor, Becky Phillips, Claire Peck, and Timothy Hardwick—lost their lives under her care. In total, Beverley attacked 13 children, leaving permanent damage to many of those who survived.

Each time an emergency struck in the ward, Beverley was often the first to respond. She would appear calm and collected, performing CPR or calling for help, which led her colleagues to see her as a dedicated and caring nurse. They praised her for her quick thinking and commitment to the children. Ironically, these very emergencies were often caused by Beverley herself. She thrived on the chaos she created, reveling in the attention she received as she "saved" her patients, even if it was she who had pushed them to the brink of death.

For a while, no one suspected her. The parents of the children trusted Beverley implicitly, never imagining that the nurse caring for their sick sons and daughters could be responsible for their sudden and unexplained illnesses. Beverley's colleagues, too, were none the wiser. Her facade of care and competence masked her true intentions so well that it took time for anyone to piece together the horrifying truth.

But as more children became critically ill or died, suspicions began to surface. The sudden spike in deaths in the children's ward raised red flags. Doctors and staff started to question whether these were truly natural tragedies or if something more sinister was at play. An investigation was launched, and the hospital's records were meticulously combed through. The disturbing pattern of Beverley's presence during each incident became undeniable.

In 1993, Beverley was arrested. The investigation uncovered a web of deceit, control, and malevolence. During her trial, the court heard harrowing details of how she had deliberately injected children with insulin, potassium, and other substances. Beverley sat silently throughout the trial, showing little emotion, her expression cold and detached. She maintained her innocence, but the overwhelming evidence against her painted a different picture. The media dubbed her "The Angel of Death."

Beverley was found guilty of four counts of murder, three counts of attempted murder, and six counts of grievous bodily harm. She was sentenced to 13 life sentences, a punishment that ensured she would never be released from prison. The judge described her crimes as "exceptionally serious" and "deeply disturbing." Her life behind bars would be spent at Rampton Secure Hospital, a psychiatric facility for those diagnosed with severe mental illness. Beverley was later diagnosed with Munchausen syndrome by proxy, a condition where caregivers cause harm to those in their care to gain attention and sympathy for themselves.

Beverley's actions sent shockwaves through the UK and the healthcare community. Hospitals across the country were forced to confront the uncomfortable reality that their screening and monitoring practices were insufficient. How had someone like Beverley Allitt slipped through the cracks? How had she been allowed to harm so many without anyone noticing for so long? The healthcare system had to change, and change it did. Hospitals reviewed their hiring procedures, implemented stricter psychological screenings, and introduced new measures to better monitor staff behavior, particularly in high-risk areas like pediatric wards.

For the families of the victims, however, no amount of reform could bring back what they had lost. The grief and trauma inflicted by Beverley's actions would last a lifetime. "We trusted her," one grieving parent said. "She was supposed to protect our children, not take them away from us." The betrayal they felt was profound. Beverley had violated the most sacred trust—that of a caregiver entrusted with the lives of children.

Beverley Allitt's legacy is one of infamy. Her name has become synonymous with betrayal, cruelty, and manipulation. The "Angel of Death" had taken on a new meaning—a woman who had used her position of trust to commit unimaginable acts of evil. Her case has been studied extensively by criminologists and psychologists, who continue to grapple with the complexities of her actions and what drove her to kill. Was it simply a need for attention, or was there something more deeply disturbed within her psyche? The answers remain elusive, but her story serves as a sobering reminder of the potential for darkness in those we trust most.

Today, Beverley Allitt is remembered as one of the UK's most notorious serial killers. Her story is a grim reminder of the importance of vigilance in the healthcare profession. While healthcare workers are often seen as heroes—and many truly are—the case of Beverley Allitt shows that not all heroes wear their true intentions on their sleeves. It is a story that forces us to question how we balance trust with oversight, and how we protect the most vulnerable members of society from those who may seek to harm them.

Beverley Allitt's actions will forever haunt the families of her victims and the broader healthcare system that failed to catch her in time. She remains a figure of horror, a stark reminder of what can happen when trust is betrayed by someone in a position of care.

8. The Poisoner's Secret

Blanche Taylor Moore was the embodiment of Southern charm, a woman known for her warm smile and deep devotion to her church. She lived her life in the rural heart of North Carolina, where people knew their neighbors by name and trusted one another without question. But beneath that carefully cultivated exterior lay a darkness that few could have imagined. Her story would shock not just her small community but the nation, revealing the terrifying possibility that someone who seemed so caring could hide such malevolence.

Blanche Kiser was born on February 17, 1933, in Concord, North Carolina. Life in the Kiser household was hard, shaped by the poverty of the Great Depression and the cruelty of her father, Parker Kiser. Parker was a violent alcoholic, and his outbursts made life unbearable for Blanche, her mother Flonnie, and her six siblings. Their small home in the humid heat of North Carolina summers became a prison of tension and fear. Blanche, like her siblings, learned to tiptoe around her father's rage, but the scars of that fear stayed with her. The desire to escape this life was imprinted deep within her.

School was a refuge for Blanche, a place where she could distance herself from her tumultuous home life. She was an average student, quiet and unremarkable in her performance, but what she lacked in academic achievement, she made up for with charm. Even at a young age, she understood how to manipulate the perceptions of others, a skill that would later serve her in deadly ways. As she grew older, her ambitions for a better life became more pronounced. She was determined to leave the hardship of her family behind and build a new life, one of security and respectability.

In 1952, Blanche married James Napoleon Taylor. On the surface, their life seemed ordinary—Blanche stayed home to care for their two children, Cindy and Steven, while James worked to support the family. But beneath the surface, their marriage was troubled. James had his own struggles, particularly with his health, and their financial situation was far from stable. Blanche, always looking for a way out, began to grow restless. Tragedy struck in 1973 when James died unexpectedly. The cause was listed as a heart attack, but whispers began to circulate, hinting at something more sinister.

Blanche, however, played the role of the grieving widow perfectly. Her charm and deep involvement in her church endeared her to the community. She sang in the choir, attended services regularly, and was seen as a pillar of faith. No one suspected that she might have played a role in her husband's death. The attention and sympathy she received seemed to give her exactly what she craved: control, power, and admiration.

After James's death, Blanche quickly moved on. She entered into relationships with other men, most notably Raymond Reid, a local businessman she had known through her work at Kroger, the grocery store where she had worked for years. Raymond was a kind man, and their relationship seemed to be progressing toward marriage. But Raymond, too, began to fall ill. It started slowly—nausea, fatigue, stomach pains. The doctors couldn't pinpoint the cause, and Raymond's condition worsened over time. Blanche, always by his side, cared for him with what seemed like devotion, but her help was anything but pure.

Raymond Reid died in 1986, and once again, Blanche found herself receiving sympathy and support from the community. It wasn't long before she began seeing Dwight Moore, a local pastor. Dwight, like the men before him, found himself falling under Blanche's spell. They were soon engaged, and just days before their wedding in 1989, Dwight fell violently ill, much like Raymond had. His body was ravaged with pain, and doctors were at a loss. But Dwight's case would prove to be different.

After extensive testing, the doctors discovered that Dwight's body was full of arsenic. The once kindly pastor had been slowly poisoned. This revelation set off a cascade of investigations, uncovering the same deadly substance in the remains of Raymond Reid and even Blanche's first husband, James Taylor. The truth was finally emerging—Blanche Taylor Moore was a serial poisoner.

Blanche's arrest in 1989 shocked everyone who knew her. The woman who had been seen as a devoted churchgoer, a loving mother, and a caring partner was now exposed as a cold-blooded killer. Her trial, held in 1990, captivated the nation. The prosecution laid out a chilling case: Blanche had used arsenic to kill not only James Taylor and Raymond Reid but had also attempted to murder Dwight Moore. There were even suspicions that she had poisoned her own father and mother-in-law.

Throughout the trial, Blanche maintained her innocence. Her soft voice and calm demeanor belied the monstrous acts she had committed. She portrayed herself as a victim of circumstance, a woman who had been unfortunate in love but certainly not a killer. "I loved them," she told the court. But the evidence against her was overwhelming. Blanche had methodically poisoned her victims, administering small doses of arsenic over time to avoid suspicion. Her meticulous approach had worked for years until Dwight's survival unraveled her deadly game.

In November 1990, Blanche was convicted of the first-degree murder of Raymond Reid and sentenced to death. The jury was unanimous in their decision, convinced by the mountain of evidence that pointed to Blanche's guilt. She was also convicted of attempting to murder Dwight Moore and suspected in the deaths of others. As the death sentence was handed down, Blanche remained stoic, her expression betraying no remorse for the lives she had taken.

Blanche Taylor Moore now sits on death row, her case a haunting reminder of how evil can hide behind a mask of kindness. Her crimes not only shattered the lives of her victims' families but also shook the community's faith in the people they trusted most. For years, Blanche had fooled those closest to her, using her charm and religious devotion to manipulate and control. She had been praised for her resilience, and her strength in the face of loss, but all the while, she had been the architect of those tragedies.

The revelations of Blanche's crimes led to significant changes in how unexplained illnesses and deaths were investigated. The case highlighted the need for better forensic practices, particularly in cases of suspected poisoning. It also served as a stark reminder that even those who seem to care for us can sometimes harbor the darkest of intentions.

Blanche's story continues to fascinate criminologists, psychologists, and true crime enthusiasts. How could someone so seemingly loving, so deeply involved in her church, commit such heinous acts? Was it the product of her abusive childhood, her need for control, or something more sinister? Her actions defy easy explanations, but they serve as a warning about the dangers of unchecked trust.

Today, Blanche Taylor Moore is remembered as one of America's most notorious female serial killers. Her name is synonymous with betrayal, manipulation, and murder. "She seemed so kind," one of her former neighbors remarked. "It's hard to reconcile the woman we knew with the crimes she committed." And that is what makes Blanche's story so terrifying—how easily she hid her evil behind a facade of kindness and faith.

Blanche's obsession with control extended beyond the poison she slipped into her victims' food. It was about maintaining the perfect image, about ensuring that those around her saw her as a loving, caring woman. Her victims never stood a chance against her manipulative charm, and by the time they realized what was happening, it was too late.

Blanche Taylor Moore's legacy is one of horror, a stark reminder of the darkness that can lie within even the most trusted individuals. Her story forces us to confront the uncomfortable truth that evil doesn't always look the way we expect. Sometimes, it wears a kind smile, sings in the church choir, and holds your hand while you die.

9. A Deadly Alliance

C arol Mary Bundy's life seemed unremarkable at first glance. Born on August 26, 1942, in Los Angeles, California, she was the second of three children in a troubled household. Her father, Charles Bundy, was an alcoholic, and her mother, Gladys, struggled with mental illness. The sunny skies of Southern California belied the storm brewing inside their home, a place where tension and fear permeated every room. Carol's childhood was marked by emotional neglect and abuse, setting the stage for the darkness that would eventually take over her life.

As a young girl, Carol craved attention. She grew up in a chaotic environment where love and affection were scarce, and her parents' frequent arguments filled her world with instability. Moving from one school to another due to her family's financial troubles, she struggled academically and socially, never quite finding her place. Despite these challenges, Carol managed to graduate from high school, but her formative years left her emotionally vulnerable, craving the approval and love she had never received at home.

Carol's relationship with her parents was strained. Her father's alcoholism turned him into an unpredictable and often violent figure, while her mother's mental instability left her distant and incapable of providing the nurturing Carol needed. Her siblings were also caught in the dysfunction, and while they shared the pain of growing up in such a household, their relationships were distant, shaped by the trauma they endured together.

Desperate for escape, Carol married young. But her hopes of finding stability and love through marriage quickly crumbled. Her first marriage ended in divorce, as did her subsequent marriages. She had two children, Cindy and Steven, but her troubled personal life made it difficult for her to care for them. More often than not, she left her children with her mother or placed them in foster care, a painful reminder of her own inability to break free from the cycle of neglect and instability she had experienced as a child.

By the late 1970s, Carol was working as a licensed vocational nurse, a career that gave her a sense of purpose. She had always enjoyed helping others, and nursing seemed like the perfect way to channel her need for approval. She found solace in her work, even as her personal life spiraled out of control. Her financial troubles and unstable relationships weighed heavily on her, but she held onto the idea that she could make something better for herself.

Everything changed when Carol met Douglas Clark in 1980. Clark was charismatic, charming, and confident—the kind of man who immediately captivated Carol. At the time, she was lonely, vulnerable, and searching for someone to give her the love and attention she had always longed for. Clark seemed to offer just that, but his influence would soon take her down a path of unimaginable violence.

Clark had a dark, twisted side, one that fascinated and terrified Carol in equal measure. He confided in her about his violent fantasies, describing his desire to murder young women. At first, Carol was horrified. She had never imagined herself capable of such things. But Clark was manipulative, preying on her insecurities and vulnerabilities. Over time, he wore down her resistance, convincing her that they could share something special if she joined him in his murderous pursuits.

Their relationship quickly spiraled into a deadly partnership, one that would later be known as the Sunset Strip Murders. Together, they lured young women into their car with promises of rides or help. Once the women were inside, Clark would sexually assault them before killing them, often shooting them at point-blank range. Carol's role in these crimes was not limited to assisting Clark—she actively participated, helping him dispose of the bodies and even encouraging his sadistic behavior.

The murders left Los Angeles in fear. Bodies of young women were being found near the Sunset Strip, and the media buzzed with speculation about the killers. No one suspected Carol, the quiet, unassuming nurse, of being involved in such horrific acts. She maintained her job, continued to read her romance novels, and kept up appearances as an ordinary woman. But behind the scenes, she was sinking deeper into a world of violence and manipulation.

One of the most chilling aspects of Carol's involvement was her transformation from reluctant accomplice to willing participant. Clark's manipulation played a significant role in this change, but there was also a darker side to Carol herself. Years of emotional neglect and abuse had left her desperate for validation, and in her twisted relationship with Clark, she found a sense of belonging, however horrific. She wanted to please him, to be loved by him, even if that meant embracing his monstrous desires.

Eventually, the weight of their crimes became too much for Carol to bear. Guilt and fear began to gnaw at her, and in August 1980, she confessed her involvement in the murders to a co-worker. The co-worker, shocked by what Carol had revealed, alerted the authorities. Carol was arrested, and the details of the Sunset Strip Murders began to unravel.

During her interrogation, Carol implicated Clark as the mastermind behind the killings. She claimed she had been manipulated, and coerced into participating in the murders. While there was some truth to her claims, it was clear that Carol had also made choices—choices that led to the deaths of innocent young women. In court, her defense team painted her as a vulnerable woman, a victim of Clark's psychological control. But the jury saw through this. Carol was not just a passive bystander—she had actively participated in the killings, and for that, she was held accountable.

In 1983, Carol Bundy was sentenced to life in prison without the possibility of parole. Douglas Clark was also convicted and sentenced to death. The public was horrified by the details of their crimes, unable to comprehend how an ordinary woman like Carol could fall so far. "She was always so quiet and unassuming," one former neighbor said. "It's hard to imagine her being involved in such horrific crimes."

The case of Carol Bundy and Douglas Clark had a profound impact on law enforcement. The Sunset Strip Murders highlighted the dangers of abusive relationships and the ease with which vulnerable individuals can be manipulated into committing terrible acts. The case also prompted discussions about the need for psychological intervention for individuals showing violent tendencies, especially those caught in toxic, controlling relationships.

In prison, Carol continued to assert that she had been coerced by Clark, that she was more victim than villain. But the evidence painted a different picture—one of a woman who had made a series of choices, driven by a deep-seated need for approval, love, and control. Carol's story became a cautionary tale about the dangers of falling under the influence of a manipulative partner, a reminder of how ordinary individuals can be drawn into extraordinary evil.

Today, Carol Bundy is remembered as one of the most infamous female accomplices in American crime history. Her story serves as a chilling reminder of the potential for violence within seemingly ordinary people and the power of manipulation in relationships. Through her life, we see how the scars of childhood abuse and emotional neglect can shape a person's choices, leading them down a path of darkness and destruction.

Though disturbing, Carol Bundy's life is an essential part of understanding the complexities of human behavior and the impact of psychological manipulation. Her story forces us to confront uncomfortable truths about trust, vulnerability, and the dangerous dynamics of abusive relationships. It serves as a haunting reminder that evil does not always present itself in obvious ways—sometimes, it hides behind a quiet smile, waiting for the right moment to strike.

10. The Darkness of Manipulation

C harlene Adell Williams was born on October 10, 1956, in Stockton, California, into a world of privilege. The only child of Charles and Mercedes Williams, Charlene grew up in a well-to-do family. Her father was a successful entrepreneur, providing her with material comforts, while her mother kept the household in order. But despite the outward appearance of wealth and stability, the warmth and affection Charlene craved were often absent from her life. Behind the sunny skies of California, the atmosphere in Charlene's home was cold, controlled by her father's high expectations.

From an early age, Charlene was burdened by the pressure to meet her parents' ambitions. Her father's strict discipline left her feeling isolated, unable to express herself. She grew up yearning for approval and love, but in the Williams household, perfection was the standard, and Charlene constantly felt like she fell short. By the time she graduated from Lodi High School in 1974, Charlene had already experienced two short-lived marriages, both of which failed to provide the escape she was seeking.

In 1977, Charlene's life changed forever when she met Gerald Gallego, a man whose presence was as overpowering as it was dangerous. He was older, charismatic, and had a dark magnetism that drew Charlene in. Gerald had a violent past, a string of arrests, and a criminal history that Charlene knew about but chose to ignore. For a young woman longing for love and acceptance, Gerald seemed like an escape from her father's control. But what Charlene didn't realize was that she was walking into an even darker form of manipulation.

They married in 1978, and almost immediately, Charlene became entwined in Gerald's deadly fantasies. He wanted something horrifying—young women he could keep as "love slaves." At first, Charlene was horrified by his desires. She couldn't imagine going along with such violence. But Gerald had a way of manipulating her, breaking her down until her reluctance was replaced by submission. He controlled her completely, and Charlene, already vulnerable, found herself doing the unthinkable just to keep his approval.

Their killing spree began in September 1978. The first victims were two teenage girls, Rhonda Scheffler and Kippi Vaught. Gerald and Charlene lured the girls into their van with the promise of giving them a ride. Once inside, the true nightmare began. Gerald sexually assaulted and murdered both girls while Charlene watched, complicit in the horror. It was the beginning of what would become a series of brutal murders that would leave ten young women and girls dead over the next two years.

Charlene's role in the killings was chilling. She became an active participant, helping Gerald lure victims by acting friendly and disarming, using her soft-spoken nature to convince the women that they were safe. Once the victims were in their clutches, Gerald's violence would unfold while Charlene assisted in disposing of the bodies. Her transformation from an unwilling accomplice to a willing participant was shocking. Under Gerald's control, her moral compass had shifted so drastically that she was capable of unimaginable cruelty.

The couple's killing spree sent waves of terror through California and Nevada. The victims—young women and teenagers—were snatched from shopping malls, parking lots, and bus stops. They were lured into what they thought were harmless situations, only to meet horrific fates. Charlene and Gerald were cunning, careful to cover their tracks, and for a time, it seemed like they might never be caught.

But in November 1980, their violent partnership came to an end. After murdering two more victims, Craig Miller and Mary Beth Sowers, the couple made a critical mistake: there were witnesses. Miller's friends had seen Charlene driving the van that abducted him, and their description of the vehicle led the police straight to the Gallegos. The arrest was swift, but what came next was a shocking unraveling of their gruesome crimes.

Charlene was arrested, and under immense pressure, she quickly turned on Gerald, cutting a deal with the authorities. In exchange for a reduced sentence, she agreed to testify against him, confessing to her role in the murders and detailing Gerald's brutal actions. Her testimony was the key to securing his conviction. While Gerald was sentenced to death, Charlene was sentenced to 16 years and 8 months in prison. It was a decision that left many questioning how someone so involved in the deaths of ten innocent people could escape the death penalty.

Charlene's trial painted a picture of a woman deeply manipulated by a violent and controlling man. She claimed that Gerald had coerced her into participating in the murders and that she had been trapped in an abusive relationship, doing whatever it took to avoid his wrath. But while Gerald's manipulation was undeniable, Charlene's complicity couldn't be ignored. She had lured the victims, driven the van, and stood by while the murders took place.

In prison, Charlene tried to rehabilitate her image. She portrayed herself as a victim of Gerald's manipulation, someone who had been swept up in his violent fantasies. But the truth was far more complex. Charlene's need for approval and her desire to please Gerald had led her to commit horrific acts. She had been manipulated, yes, but she had also made choices.

One of the most disturbing aspects of Charlene's transformation was how her need for control and approval fed into her role in the murders. The woman who had once loved music and played the piano now found herself an accomplice in Gerald's sadistic world. Her earlier love for animals and her quiet hobbies seemed like distant memories, replaced by a chilling willingness to do whatever it took to keep Gerald happy.

When Gerald was sentenced to death, the courtroom buzzed with a sense of closure. But for the families of the victims, the pain would never fully go away. Charlene's cooperation with authorities had saved her from a similar fate, but it hadn't erased the devastation she had helped cause. For the rest of her life, Charlene would carry the weight of her crimes.

Charlene Gallego's story is a complex one, steeped in manipulation, fear, and personal responsibility. Her relationship with Gerald wasn't just abusive—it was a dark spiral into evil, a descent that saw her become an active participant in the violent destruction of innocent lives. Today, Charlene Gallego is remembered not just as an accomplice to a serial killer but as a woman who, through her desperation for love and control, allowed herself to be drawn into a deadly partnership.

Her case remains a stark reminder of the dangers of manipulation, how abusive relationships can distort a person's sense of morality, and the horrifying consequences that can follow. Charlene's legacy is one of infamy, a cautionary tale of how vulnerability and fear can lead ordinary individuals into extraordinary acts of evil.

11. A Nurse's Dark Choices

C hristine Malevre's story is one of compassion twisted by desperation, a nurse whose good intentions veered into darkness. Born on January 10, 1970, in Mantes-la-Jolie, France, she seemed destined for a respectable and meaningful career in healthcare. Christine grew up in a stable, middle-class family, the eldest of three children. Her parents, both hardworking professionals, raised her in a nurturing environment. Her childhood was filled with warm summers and mild winters, a peaceful contrast to the storm that would later take over her life.

From a young age, Christine was taught the values of responsibility and care. As the eldest, she helped raise her younger siblings, often stepping into a maternal role. The admiration for her mother's work as a nurse inspired her to follow in her footsteps. After excelling in school, Christine pursued nursing, entering a profession where compassion, care, and duty to others were central values. But no one could have predicted how those values would become dangerously distorted.

By the mid-1990s, Christine had secured a position at the François-Quesnay Hospital in her hometown of Mantes-la-Jolie, working in the palliative care unit. This was where the terminally ill came to find comfort in their final days, and it was here that Christine's perspective on life and death began to change. Each day, she watched patients suffer, their bodies ravaged by illness, their pain so unbearable that even medication couldn't help them. The weight of their suffering began to take a toll on her.

Christine often sat by their bedsides, holding their hands, listening to their fears, and feeling helpless. "I couldn't bear to see them suffer anymore," she would later explain in court, her voice trembling with emotion. She believed that her role as a nurse was not just to care for them but to spare them from the agony that came with their terminal conditions. But instead of following legal and ethical protocols, Christine started to believe that only she could decide when their pain should end.

In 1997, Christine crossed a line she could never step back from. She began administering lethal doses of medication to her patients—people she believed were suffering too much to continue living. Her first patient was a man in his late seventies, riddled with cancer. His moans of pain haunted her. She claimed that she acted out of mercy, convinced that she was offering him peace. With a quick injection, his suffering ceased. To the outside world, it appeared as though the patient had succumbed naturally to his illness. No one suspected a thing.

Over the next year, Christine repeated this act several times. She carefully chose patients who were terminally ill, and those who had no chance of recovery. Each time she ended a life, she felt both the relief of alleviating suffering and the burden of guilt weighing down on her conscience. "I thought I was helping them," she later said. "I never wanted to harm anyone."

Christine's mental state began to unravel as she carried the weight of these decisions. She was torn between the belief that she was sparing her patients from pain and the realization that what she was doing was not only illegal but deeply unethical. The internal conflict consumed her. At night, she would lie awake, haunted by the faces of those she had sent to their deaths. Yet, by day, she would walk through the hospital corridors, outwardly the same dedicated nurse, always ready to comfort those in need.

Her colleagues, unaware of what was happening behind the scenes, admired her compassion. One fellow nurse later recalled, "Christine was always the one who would sit with patients for hours, talk to their families, and offer whatever comfort she could. We had no idea what she was doing." But as Christine's actions escalated, rumors began to spread. The deaths in her ward seemed too frequent, too convenient.

In 1998, the truth began to unravel. A series of unusual deaths in the palliative care unit caught the attention of hospital administrators. An internal investigation was launched, and the suspicions quickly zeroed in on Christine. When questioned, her calm facade crumbled. She confessed to her role in the deaths of several patients, claiming she had only done it to ease their suffering. But the law saw things differently.

Christine was arrested, and charged with multiple counts of murder. Her trial became a national sensation in France, not only because of the nature of her crimes but because it reignited the long-standing debate over euthanasia. Was Christine a compassionate caregiver who had overstepped her boundaries, or was she a murderer who had taken the law into her own hands? The country was divided. Some saw her as a misguided hero, while others viewed her as a cold-blooded killer.

In court, Christine's defense argued that she had been trying to help and that she had only acted out of love for her patients. But the prosecution painted a different picture—a nurse who had crossed ethical lines, whose desire to play God had led to the deaths of innocent people. "No one asked her to end their lives," the prosecutor said. "She took that decision upon herself."

Throughout the trial, Christine remained stoic. She admitted to the killings but insisted that her intentions had been pure. "I only wanted to help them," she said again and again, her voice trembling with emotion. But the court was unsympathetic. While her actions may have been driven by compassion, they were also illegal. Christine was convicted and sentenced to 10 years in prison, a punishment that many saw as too lenient given the gravity of her crimes.

The case of Christine Malevre left a lasting mark on French society. Her actions prompted widespread discussions about euthanasia and the ethical dilemmas faced by healthcare providers. Should healthcare professionals have the right to end the lives of terminally ill patients if they believe it to be an act of mercy? Where should the line be drawn between compassion and murder? These were questions that France—and the world—had to grapple with in the wake of Christine's trial.

The legal consequences of Christine's actions led to stricter regulations in the medical field. Hospitals across France introduced more rigorous protocols for end-of-life care, ensuring that decisions about life and death were made collectively by medical teams and families, not by individual healthcare providers. The case also highlighted the need for psychological support for nurses and doctors working in palliative care, who are often exposed to immense emotional pressure.

Today, Christine Malevre's name is remembered with a mix of horror and pity. She was a woman who, by all accounts, entered the nursing profession to help people, to care for them in their most vulnerable moments. But somewhere along the way, her sense of duty became distorted. She believed she was doing the right thing, but in doing so, she crossed a line that should never have been crossed.

Christine's legacy is a complex one. While her intentions may have been rooted in compassion, her actions serve as a reminder of the dangers of taking the law into one's own hands, especially in the world of healthcare. Her story continues to be taught in medical ethics courses across the globe, a cautionary tale about the importance of adhering to legal and ethical standards, no matter how difficult the circumstances may be.

Reflecting on her actions, Christine once said, "I never wanted to harm anyone. I wanted to help them, to ease their pain." But in the end, the help she thought she was giving came at too high a price—the lives of those she had sworn to care for.

12. A Mother's Nightmare

Dagmar Johanne Amalie Overbye's name is forever etched in the dark pages of Danish history, her actions so horrifying that they changed the nation's laws on childcare and adoption forever. Born on April 23, 1887, in the quiet village of Assendrup, near Horsens, Denmark, Dagmar's early life was marked by poverty. The Overbye family, with eleven children, struggled to survive, and young Dagmar quickly learned the harsh realities of life. The cold winters of Denmark mirrored the emotional chill that filled her childhood home. Her parents, Peter and Inger, were preoccupied with putting food on the table, leaving little room for warmth or affection. For Dagmar, life was a continuous battle for survival, with no one to nurture her or show her kindness.

Growing up in such an environment shaped Dagmar in ways that no one could have predicted. She attended the village school, receiving the basic education expected for a girl in her social standing. But with no real opportunities and limited prospects, her future seemed bleak. The village, like her family, offered little in terms of escape from the grinding cycle of poverty. As a young woman, Dagmar drifted through a series of failed relationships, each leaving her more isolated and desperate than the last.

Her first child was born out of wedlock, a scandalous situation in early 20th-century Denmark. The child's death shortly after birth was suspicious, but no one questioned it deeply at the time. Soon after, she married and had another baby, but this child also died under unclear circumstances. The whispers around her began to grow, but Dagmar was skilled at hiding the truth behind a veneer of respectability. She presented herself as a hardworking woman, struggling under the weight of unfortunate circumstances, but beneath this facade lurked a woman capable of unimaginable cruelty.

Dagmar found her calling in baby farming, a practice where women took in infants from unwed mothers or families who couldn't care for their children. In the early 1900s, such arrangements were common in Denmark, with few regulations and even fewer safeguards to protect the children. For many desperate mothers, Dagmar appeared to be a savior, offering care and a future for their unwanted babies. But instead of caring for the infants, Dagmar found a more sinister way to profit.

She quickly realized that the children were worth more to her dead than alive. Keeping them meant feeding, clothing, and sheltering them, which was expensive. Killing them, however, allowed her to collect the money from their mothers without the burden of caring for them. And so, between 1913 and 1920, Dagmar systematically murdered at least nine infants, though many believe the real number may have been higher.

Her methods were cold and brutal. She would either strangle the babies or drown them, disposing of their tiny bodies in stoves or burying them in shallow graves. She worked quickly and efficiently, never showing remorse or hesitation. Each life she ended was just another transaction, another way to survive in a world that had always been cruel to her. But no one suspected her. Dagmar was clever, maintaining her outward appearance as a responsible caretaker. She dressed well, attended social events, and kept a respectable distance from any rumors that might taint her reputation. It was this very facade that allowed her to continue her killing spree undetected for years.

Her emotional state during this period remains a mystery. Did she feel guilt, or had she buried her conscience so deep that she no longer felt anything at all? Dagmar's stoicism throughout her trial would later suggest a woman utterly detached from the suffering she caused. But it's clear that her early life of deprivation, coupled with her failed relationships and the societal stigma of being an unwed mother, had hardened her. The survival instincts she developed in her youth had twisted into something monstrous.

By 1920, Dagmar's dark secret was on the verge of unraveling. A mother, anxious about the fate of her baby, demanded to know where her child was. When Dagmar couldn't provide a satisfactory answer, the authorities were alerted. The investigation that followed uncovered a chilling pattern of disappearances, leading directly to Dagmar's doorstep. When the police arrived, they found the remains of infants hidden in her home, a discovery that sent shockwaves through the country.

The trial that followed was one of the most sensational in Danish history. Newspapers plastered Dagmar's face across their front pages, and her name became synonymous with evil. During the proceedings, Dagmar showed little emotion, calmly describing her crimes as if they were just another part of her day-to-day life. "I didn't want them to suffer," she claimed in a rare moment of explanation, but there was no sympathy for her. The public was horrified by the extent of her cruelty, especially towards the most vulnerable members of society—infants who had no way of defending themselves.

One of the most chilling aspects of the trial was Dagmar's complete lack of remorse. Her detachment from the enormity of her actions was unsettling. She had convinced herself, it seemed, that the deaths were somehow necessary, a twisted solution to her financial problems. But the court saw her for what she was—a ruthless murderer. Dagmar was found guilty of nine counts of murder and sentenced to death, though her sentence was later commuted to life in prison. She spent the rest of her days behind bars, dying in 1929, alone and forgotten.

But Dagmar Overbye's legacy did not end with her death. Her crimes led to a national outcry, forcing Denmark to reform its childcare and adoption laws. The lax regulations that had allowed Dagmar to operate for so long were tightened, and stricter oversight was introduced to protect children. No longer could someone like Dagmar slip through the cracks, preying on the vulnerable without consequences.

The reforms included more rigorous background checks for those involved in childcare and better tracking of adopted and fostered children. Dagmar's case became a touchstone for discussions on child welfare, both in Denmark and internationally. Her actions had revealed the dark underbelly of a system that had failed to protect those who needed it most.

Today, Dagmar Overbye is remembered as one of Denmark's most notorious serial killers. Her name still evokes a sense of horror, a reminder of how someone entrusted with the care of children could exploit that trust in the worst possible way. She remains a figure of fascination in criminology and social work studies, her case is used as an example of the dangers of unchecked power in childcare.

One of Dagmar's surviving relatives once described her as "a monster disguised as a savior." It was a fitting description for a woman who hid her murderous intentions behind a mask of respectability. She had fooled everyone, from the desperate mothers who handed over their babies to the authorities who had taken so long to uncover her crimes. But in the end, Dagmar's greed and lack of empathy led to her downfall.

Her story, though deeply disturbing, serves as a crucial reminder of the need for constant vigilance in protecting children. It also sheds light on the darker aspects of human nature—how a person's circumstances, combined with desperation and a lack of empathy, can lead to unspeakable acts of cruelty. Dagmar Overbye's life is a chilling example of how even the most ordinary of individuals can harbor extraordinary evil, and her legacy continues to shape the way society views and safeguards the vulnerable.

13. The Charm of Darkness

D ana Sue Gray's life was a story of unsettling contrasts, a descent from a seemingly normal existence into the abyss of violence and murder. Born on December 6, 1957, in sunny southern California, she was raised in a middle-class family. Her father, Russell Armbrust, was a hairdresser, and her mother, Beverly Arnett, was a former beauty queen. But while the California weather was warm and bright, Dana's early life was anything but.

Dana grew up in a home full of tension. Her parents' marriage was fraught with arguments, and eventually, they divorced when Dana was still young. The separation left a mark on Dana, who was already known for her rebellious nature. Her relationship with her mother, Beverly, was especially strained. Beverly's expectations weighed heavily on Dana, and their clashes became frequent. Dana felt immense pressure to live up to her mother's standards but struggled to find her own path in life. Her father's remarriage and subsequent distance only deepened her sense of abandonment.

As a teenager in Newport Beach, Dana had an outgoing personality and striking looks. But beneath the surface, she was struggling. Her academic performance in high school was mediocre at best, and she often skipped classes. Despite her difficulties, Dana graduated and chose a career in nursing, perhaps hoping to bring care and healing to others in a way she couldn't find in her own life. Nursing seemed to be the one constant in her life—a profession built on compassion and responsibility.

Dana's career started well. She showed promise as a nurse, earning praise from her patients and colleagues. But her personal life was falling apart. She married and divorced twice, both marriages ending bitterly. Her second husband, Tom Gray, shared her love of adventure sports, but even their shared passion couldn't save their marriage. As the years went by, Dana found herself increasingly isolated. She had no children, no stable relationships, and mounting financial pressures.

Dana's hobbies were an escape. She loved skydiving and windsurfing, thrill-seeking activities that gave her a rush of excitement and a sense of control. But her love for expensive tastes and lavish shopping sprees led to debt. The financial instability worsened over time, and Dana found herself unable to

46

keep up with her mounting bills. This financial desperation, combined with her deep sense of isolation and bitterness, became the catalyst for her spiral into darkness.

The key turning point came in the early 1990s when Dana's financial struggles and personal despair reached their peak. It was then that she began plotting a series of cold-blooded murders. Her first known victim was Norma Davis, an elderly woman who lived alone in Dana's neighborhood. Dana had known Norma through her stepmother, making it easy for her to gain the older woman's trust. On February 16, 1994, Dana entered Norma's home, brutally strangled her with a phone cord, and stabbed her. Dana left the house with jewelry and other valuables, sparking what would become a series of chilling crimes.

Dana's method was terrifyingly consistent. She targeted elderly women, all of whom lived alone. Her next victim was June Roberts, another older woman Dana knew personally. On February 28, 1994, Dana entered June's home under the guise of visiting a friend. Once inside, she attacked June, strangling her with a phone cord just as she had done to Norma. Dana then stole June's credit cards, which she used to fund a shopping spree. Her need for financial gain fueled her violence, and each murder became a way to satisfy both her greed and her growing sense of control over life and death.

Her third known victim was Dorinda Hawkins, who miraculously survived Dana's attack. On March 10, 1994, Dana entered Dorinda's workplace and offered to give her a ride home. Once they were alone, Dana attempted to strangle her. Dorinda barely escaped with her life, and her testimony would later become crucial in Dana's arrest and conviction. But Dana's spree didn't stop there.

On March 16, Dana struck again, killing 87-year-old Winifred Johnson. The violence in her attacks was escalating, with each crime becoming more brutal than the last. But Dana's luck was about to run out. After leaving a trail of blood and terror, Dana was arrested on March 18, 1994, while out on another shopping spree using her victims' stolen credit cards.

The arrest of Dana Sue Gray shocked her friends and neighbors, many of whom couldn't reconcile the friendly, vivacious woman they knew with the cold-blooded killer revealed in the media. One former acquaintance said, "She always had a smile, but you never knew what was behind it." Another described her as "charming and vivacious," a description that seemed impossible to reconcile with the person responsible for such horrific crimes.

Dana's trial became a media spectacle. As one of the few female serial killers in American history, her case drew widespread attention. During the trial, Dana showed little remorse, calmly detailing her actions with a chilling lack of emotion. Her defense argued that her financial desperation and mental instability had driven her to kill, but the jury was not swayed. Dana was convicted of multiple counts of murder and sentenced to life imprisonment without the possibility of parole.

While Dana claimed she killed out of desperation, her crimes revealed a darker truth: a complete lack of empathy for her victims. She had taken advantage of the trust these elderly women had placed in her, using her charm and appearance to lure them into a false sense of security before violently ending their lives. The contrast between her public persona as a friendly, adventurous woman and her private reality as a ruthless killer left many struggling to understand how such darkness could exist in someone who seemed so normal.

Dana's actions had a profound impact on society. Her crimes highlighted the vulnerabilities of elderly individuals living alone, leading to increased awareness and protection for this vulnerable population. Her case also prompted discussions about the need for better safeguards in caregiving roles and a deeper understanding of the warning signs of psychopathy in seemingly ordinary people.

Even years after her conviction, Dana Sue Gray remains a chilling figure in the annals of American crime. Her story is often referenced in criminology and psychology courses as a case study of the complexities of human behavior and the potential for violence hidden beneath the surface of normalcy. She serves as a reminder of the darkness that can lie beneath even the most charming and outwardly successful individuals.

One lesser-known fact about Dana is how easily she could blend into society, using her looks and charm to manipulate those around her. This ability to move seamlessly between her public and private lives made her actions all the more shocking when they were finally revealed. Her life serves as a stark example of how desperation, isolation, and a skewed sense of entitlement can lead to unimaginable acts of violence.

Dana's legacy is one of infamy and tragedy. Her actions forever scarred the lives of her victims' families and left a lasting impact on society's understanding of female violence and serial killers. What made her infamous was not just the brutal nature of her crimes but her ability to hide her deadly intentions behind a mask of charm and normalcy. Her story remains a powerful reminder of the duality of human nature and the need for vigilance in protecting the most vulnerable among us.

Through Dana Sue Gray's life, we see the complexities of human behavior and the dangerous consequences of unresolved emotional trauma, financial desperation, and unchecked greed. Her story, while deeply unsettling, provides valuable insights into the darker sides of human nature and the importance of addressing mental health and societal safeguards to prevent such tragedies from happening again.

14. The Noble Killer

Darya Nikolayevna Saltykova, often referred to as "Saltychikha," was born into the world of luxury and power, but her name would be remembered for cruelty and violence. Born on March 11, 1730, in Russia, she grew up surrounded by wealth. Her father, Nikolai Avtonomovich Ivanov, was a respected nobleman, and her mother, Anna Ivanovna Davydova, came from a prominent family. The estates of 18th-century Russia, where Darya was raised, were marked by the vastness of the lands, the lavish homes, and the stark difference between the privileged nobility and the suffering serfs.

Darya's childhood was one of privilege. She was educated in French, taught to play the piano, and schooled in the elegant manners expected of a noblewoman. She hosted grand dinners and was expected to carry herself with dignity. But there were early signs of cruelty that went unnoticed or were brushed aside due to her status. As a child, she had a violent temper and little empathy. There was a darkness growing inside her, one that would later erupt in unimaginable cruelty.

Her marriage to Gleb Alexeyevich Saltykov, another nobleman, came at a young age. It was a typical arranged marriage, where love was secondary to the merging of two powerful families. They had two sons, Theodore and Nicholas, but her husband's untimely death in 1755 left Darya a widow at just twenty-five. She was now the sole manager of their vast estates, including hundreds of serfs who worked the land. In the absence of her husband, Darya's darker tendencies began to emerge.

Her authority over the serfs became absolute, and with that power, her cruelty intensified. Managing the estate was a burden, and Darya began taking out her frustrations on the serfs under her command, especially the women. The serfs were seen as property, with no rights or protection from the abuses of their masters. It was within this system that Darya found a sickening sense of control and pleasure. She beat them, tortured them, and often killed them.

What began as harsh punishments soon turned into a terrifying pattern of violence. Darya was known for flying into fits of rage over the smallest inconveniences. A poorly cleaned floor, a missed task—any slight mistake was enough to unleash her wrath. She would order the women to be beaten to the brink of death or sometimes kill them herself. Witnesses would later describe how she took pleasure in the suffering, watching her victims writhe in agony as she inflicted pain.

Her methods of torture were brutal. Some victims were starved, others were beaten with iron rods or tortured for days. She was known to mutilate her victims' bodies, displaying an extreme disregard for human life. Many of the young women died slow and painful deaths, their cries for mercy ignored by the woman who saw herself as untouchable. To Darya, these women were nothing more than tools, and their lives were hers to take.

The estate, once grand and serene, now had a dark and fearful atmosphere. The serfs lived in constant terror, knowing that any mistake could be their last. Darya's cruelty knew no bounds, and there was no one to stop her. Despite rumors of her brutality spreading, no one dared to confront her. She was a noblewoman, after all, and in 18th-century Russia, the nobility was practically immune to the law.

Her reign of terror lasted for years, and it is believed that Darya tortured and killed more than 100 serfs, mostly young women. These victims often came from impoverished families, and their deaths went unreported because no one dared challenge a woman of such power. The silence surrounding her crimes only added to her belief that she could continue her murderous spree without consequence.

But as the bodies piled up, whispers grew louder. Some brave serfs, despite the fear of retaliation, gathered enough courage to petition Empress Catherine the Great, pleading for justice. By then, the stories of Darya's cruelty were impossible to ignore, and in 1762, Catherine ordered an investigation. Even for a powerful noble like Darya, the pressure from the Empress was impossible to escape.

When the investigators arrived at her estate, they found overwhelming evidence of her crimes. The testimonies from the surviving serfs painted a grim picture of life under Darya's rule. One witness described her as a "monster in noble clothes," while another said, "She killed as easily as she breathed." The testimonies spoke of unimaginable suffering, and the brutality of her actions shocked even those who were used to the harsh conditions of serfdom.

Darya was arrested and put on trial for her crimes. The trial was a sensation in Russian society, as it was one of the first instances where a noble was publicly held accountable for the abuse of power. The case exposed the widespread mistreatment of serfs and the dangers of unchecked authority. Darya, once a figure of respect and wealth, now stood before the courts as a symbol of cruelty.

Throughout her trial, Darya remained emotionless. She did not deny the charges, nor did she show any remorse for the lives she had taken. Her cold demeanor only added to the horror of her actions. Empress Catherine the Great, who took a personal interest in the case, was appalled by what she had uncovered. "Her actions," the Empress would later say, "were inhuman and detestable."

The court found Darya guilty of the murders and sentenced her to life imprisonment. Though many called for her execution, Catherine decided to commute the sentence to life in solitary confinement, where Darya would live out her remaining years, far removed from the luxury and power she had once enjoyed. Her confinement took place in a convent in Moscow, where she spent her days in silence, cut off from the world she once terrorized. She died in 1801, at the age of 71, a prisoner of her own cruelty.

The impact of Darya's crimes on Russian society was profound. Her trial shed light on the abuses of the nobility and the need for legal reforms to protect the serfs. While it would take several more decades before serfdom was abolished in Russia, Darya's case played a role in starting the conversation about the rights of serfs and the responsibilities of the ruling class. Empress Catherine used the case as an example of why reforms were needed to ensure justice for all subjects, regardless of their status.

One lesser-known fact about Darya was her cruelty extended beyond humans. She was known to torture animals for amusement, another disturbing aspect of her sadistic personality. This behavior only further solidified the belief that Darya had no empathy for life, whether human or animal. Her heart, hardened by her sense of superiority and absolute power, was beyond redemption.

Darya Saltykova's life is a reminder of the darkness that can grow within those who hold unchecked power. Her actions, driven by a need for control and a complete disregard for life, revealed the worst aspects of human nature. She is remembered today not as a noblewoman, but as a serial killer who used her position to commit heinous acts against those who had no way to fight back.

Her story is one of cruelty, but it also serves as a powerful example of the importance of justice and accountability. Even in a world where the powerful seemed untouchable, Darya's downfall proved that no one is above the law. Her legacy is one of infamy, a dark chapter in Russian history that continues to remind us of the dangers of unchecked authority and the necessity of protecting the vulnerable.

15. The Deceptive Life

Dorothea Montalvo Puente was a woman of contradictions. Outwardly, she appeared to be a kind-hearted, elderly landlady who took care of vulnerable tenants in her Sacramento boarding house. But behind this facade lurked a cold-blooded serial killer, who exploited and murdered the very people who trusted her. Born as Dorothea Helen Gray on January 9, 1929, in Redlands, California, her early years were marked by instability and loss, which would shape the darker path her life would later take.

Her childhood was far from ideal. Dorothea's parents, Trudy Mae and Jesse James Gray, were alcoholics, struggling to keep their family afloat. The family home was a tense place, filled with the kind of instability that leaves scars. When Dorothea was just eight years old, her father died of tuberculosis, leaving the family even more adrift. Her mother passed away in a motorcycle accident soon after, orphaning Dorothea and her siblings. The young girl found herself placed in an orphanage, a place that was cold and indifferent. These early experiences of neglect and abandonment laid the groundwork for the manipulative and deceptive behavior she would display in her later years.

By the time Dorothea reached adulthood, she had become skilled at surviving. She married Fred McFaul in 1945, and they had two daughters, but Dorothea gave both children up for adoption. The marriage quickly fell apart, and Dorothea began to bounce from one relationship to another, always seeking financial stability but never finding true emotional fulfillment. She married several more times, each marriage ending in divorce, and each time she sank deeper into financial instability.

In her youth, Dorothea worked a string of odd jobs, including as a nurse's aide, but her career was marred by legal troubles. She was arrested multiple times for petty crimes like forgery and theft, but it was her cunning ability to manipulate and deceive that kept her from being truly punished for her actions. Despite her criminal past, she managed to maintain an image of respectability, presenting herself as a sweet, grandmotherly figure who loved to cook, garden, and help those in need. But beneath this exterior was a woman driven by a desire for money and power, willing to go to extreme lengths to get what she wanted.

Her first significant step into her criminal career came when she opened a boarding house in Sacramento in the 1980s. The tenants she attracted were often elderly or disabled, people with nowhere else to go. To the outside world, Dorothea was doing a noble service, providing care and shelter for those in need. But in reality, she had found the perfect cover for her darkest impulses. These tenants, many of whom were collecting social security checks, became easy targets for Dorothea's scheme.

The turning point in Dorothea's life came when she realized that she could exploit these vulnerable individuals for financial gain. She began drugging her tenants, overdosing them with sleeping pills, which often resulted in their deaths. She would then forge their signatures and continue cashing their social security checks, collecting money from the dead as if they were still alive. To keep up appearances, Dorothea would tell neighbors and officials that the tenants had moved away or checked into a hospital, ensuring no one came looking for them.

One of the most chilling aspects of Dorothea's crimes was how meticulously she covered her tracks. After killing her tenants, she buried their bodies in her backyard, ensuring they were out of sight and out of mind. Her boarding house, once filled with life, now became a graveyard for the people she had exploited and murdered. The serene garden where she once invited friends to admire her flowers was, in reality, the final resting place for her victims.

For several years, Dorothea managed to evade suspicion. Neighbors found her charming, a seemingly harmless old woman who volunteered at local charities and loved to bake. But her charm was just another tool in her manipulative arsenal. She kept up the pretense of being a caring landlady, fooling those around her while continuing her killing spree.

In 1988, Dorothea's carefully constructed world began to unravel. The police started investigating after one of her tenants, Alvaro "Bert" Montoya, a mentally disabled man, went missing. Social workers, who had grown suspicious of Bert's sudden disappearance, notified the authorities. When the police arrived at Dorothea's house to investigate, they were greeted by the seemingly sweet old woman, who denied knowing anything about Bert's whereabouts. But their suspicions grew, and soon, they began searching the property.

What they found was horrifying. As officers dug up Dorothea's yard, they discovered the remains of seven bodies buried beneath her carefully tended flowerbeds. Each discovery sent shockwaves through the community, which had previously regarded Dorothea as a beloved figure. How could someone who appeared so kind commit such monstrous acts?

The investigation revealed the extent of Dorothea's crimes. For years, she had been systematically killing her tenants and stealing their money, exploiting their trust and vulnerability for personal gain. She had chosen her victims carefully—elderly, disabled, and often without close family ties, ensuring no one would notice if they suddenly disappeared. Her cold calculation and ability to maintain a facade of innocence made her crimes all the more disturbing.

Dorothea was arrested, and her trial became a media sensation. The contrast between her sweet grandmotherly appearance and the gruesome nature of her crimes captured the nation's attention. During the trial, she continued to deny her involvement in the murders, insisting that she had not killed anyone. "I'm not guilty. I didn't kill anyone," she claimed, despite the overwhelming evidence against her. Her calm, matter-of-fact demeanor during the trial only added to the public's horror. How could someone so seemingly ordinary be capable of such evil?

In 1993, Dorothea Puente was convicted of three murders and sentenced to life in prison without the possibility of parole. She remained unrepentant until she died in 2011, never admitting to the full extent of her crimes. Even in prison, she maintained the same manipulative charm, befriending fellow inmates and guards alike.

The aftermath of Dorothea's crimes had far-reaching effects. Her case raised awareness about the vulnerability of elderly and disabled individuals, particularly those living in care facilities or dependent on others for support. It highlighted the need for stricter regulations and oversight in boarding houses and care homes, ensuring that those responsible for the care of vulnerable populations are held accountable.

Today, Dorothea Puente's name is remembered as a symbol of deceit and exploitation. Her boarding house, once a place of shelter, became a house of horrors, where the most vulnerable were preyed upon by the very person they trusted. Her legacy is one of infamy, a reminder of the darkness that can lurk beneath a facade of kindness and respectability.

What made Dorothea Puente truly terrifying was her ability to hide in plain sight. She used her grandmotherly persona to gain trust, while beneath the surface, she was committing unspeakable acts. Her story serves as a grim warning about the dangers of unchecked power and the need for vigilance in protecting those who are most vulnerable.

Through Dorothea Puente's life, we see the destructive power of manipulation and greed. Her story is a chilling reminder that evil can wear many faces, and it is often those who seem the least likely who are capable of the most heinous crimes.

16. The Chilling Story

Elfriede Blauensteiner, often known as the "Black Widow," left behind a legacy of horror and deception in Austria. Her life was a web of lies, manipulation, and greed, where she preyed on the most vulnerable, all in the pursuit of financial gain. Beneath the facade of an ordinary woman lay a calculated serial killer, whose actions shocked Austria in the 1990s.

Born on January 22, 1931, in the heart of Vienna, Elfriede grew up in difficult circumstances. That winter, the city was blanketed in snow, creating a cold and serene atmosphere, one that mirrored the hard reality of her upbringing. Her parents, Peter and Ingeborg, were modest laborers, working tirelessly to keep the family afloat. They lived in a cramped apartment in a working-class neighborhood, where the walls often echoed the tensions of financial struggle. From an early age, Elfriede learned to navigate the harsh realities of life, developing a quiet but determined personality.

Her childhood, while marked by economic difficulties, also introduced her to the charm and beauty of Vienna's cultural landscape. As a child, she wandered the streets of Vienna, marveling at the historical buildings, the elegant cafés, and the bustling markets. Yet, beneath this love for her city, Elfriede harbored a growing sense of dissatisfaction. She was always aware of the disparity between her family's modest means and the wealth of others, which ignited a desire within her to climb out of poverty.

Elfriede attended school like any other child, but her education was cut short. The need to support her struggling family became too great, and she left school early to work. This sense of responsibility, thrust upon her at a young age, nurtured her resourcefulness, but it also bred resentment. Elfriede wanted more, and as she grew older, her ambitions took a darker turn.

In her early twenties, she married a man named Friedrich. The marriage was far from happy, and it dissolved in divorce soon after. Her second marriage, to Josef Blauensteiner, brought more stability but was no less tumultuous. Josef was kind but weak-willed, and Elfriede's controlling nature became the dominant force in their relationship. The couple had one son, but Elfriede's relationship with him was strained. Her son grew up feeling the pressure of her manipulative tendencies, and they eventually became estranged.

Elfriede's early life had given her little hope or support. There were no positive mentors to guide her and no stable home environment to nurture her better instincts. Instead, she learned to rely on herself, sharpening her manipulative skills to survive and get what she wanted. It was a skill she would later use in far more sinister ways.

In the 1980s, after the death of her second husband, Elfriede discovered that there were far more lucrative ways to survive than petty theft and fraud, crimes she had already dabbled in. She realized that by befriending wealthy but lonely individuals, particularly the elderly, she could manipulate them into changing their wills in her favor. Once their assets were secured, she poisoned them, ensuring that she would inherit their wealth.

Her first known victim was an elderly man who lived alone, vulnerable, and without close family. Elfriede visited him frequently, offering help and companionship. To the outside world, she appeared as a caring neighbor, always ready with a smile or a home-cooked meal. But her kindness was a mask. Slowly, she began administering small doses of poison, making sure the man's health deteriorated. She waited patiently until he was too weak to notice her stealing his money, forging his will, and finally ending his life.

Elfriede's method was always calculated. She used Rohypnol, a potent sedative, to drug her victims, ensuring their deaths appeared natural. After their passing, she took control of their assets, living off their savings while moving on to her next target. Her victims were chosen carefully—those who had little family and whose deaths would raise few suspicions. Her manipulation was masterful; she could charm anyone into trusting her, only to betray them most cruelly.

For years, she evaded suspicion, her crimes hidden behind her pleasant demeanor. Neighbors saw her as a quiet, responsible woman who kept to herself. She spent her days knitting, gardening, and maintaining the appearance of normalcy. No one could have imagined the horrors she was hiding behind the walls of her home. But the truth was far more chilling—Elfriede was a predator, stalking her next victim with cold efficiency.

Her undoing came in the 1990s when the suspicious death of one of her victims led to an investigation. The family of the deceased had noticed strange behavior from Elfriede in the weeks leading up to the death, and the police were called. What they uncovered shocked Austria. As the investigation progressed, it became clear that Elfriede had been systematically murdering her victims for years, using their money to maintain her lifestyle while her dark secret remained hidden.

When questioned, Elfriede showed no remorse. She insisted that she had done what was necessary to survive, never once admitting to the full extent of her crimes. "I only did what was necessary to survive," she said coldly during her interrogation as if survival justified murder. Her lack of empathy, combined with her calm and collected manner, horrified those who knew her. Friends and neighbors could not reconcile the sweet old woman they had known with the monster revealed in the media.

Elfriede was tried and convicted of several murders, though authorities believe the actual number of her victims could be higher. Her trial was a media sensation, with the press dubbing her the "Black Widow." The courtroom was packed with onlookers eager to catch a glimpse of the woman who had managed to fool so many for so long. She was sentenced to life in prison, where she died in 2003.

Elfriede's story raised important questions about the vulnerability of the elderly and the dangers of unchecked trust. Her case led to calls for greater oversight in social services, particularly in the management of wills and estates for elderly individuals. It also highlighted the importance of vigilance within communities, ensuring that those most at risk are protected from those who seek to exploit them.

Elfriede Blauensteiner's legacy is one of manipulation, greed, and murder. Her crimes serve as a grim reminder of the potential for darkness within even the most unassuming individuals. Her ability to charm and deceive those around her, all while committing heinous acts of murder, has left a lasting impact on Austrian society and criminal history.

Her story is often studied in criminology and psychology courses as an example of the extremes of human behavior. The "Black Widow" is a stark symbol of the dangers of unchecked power and the capacity for evil that can exist beneath the surface of everyday life.

In the end, Elfriede Blauensteiner's name became synonymous with deceit and cruelty. She was a woman who lived two lives—one of a seemingly harmless widow and one of a cold-blooded killer. Her story is a reminder that evil can sometimes wear the most familiar and unthreatening faces, lurking behind a smile or a kind gesture.

17. The Blood Countess of Hungary

Elizabeth Bathory, often called the "Blood Countess," stands as one of history's most infamous figures. Born into the powerful Bathory family, her life seemed destined for privilege and influence. However, her name would later be associated with some of the darkest acts in European history. Her alleged crimes—torturing and killing young girls in her castles—remain a haunting tale, a legacy of cruelty and unchecked power.

Elizabeth Bathory was born on August 7, 1560, in the small town of Nyírbátor, Hungary. The lush green fields of summer stretched across the Hungarian countryside as she entered a world of wealth and status. Her father, George Bathory, was a prominent soldier, and her mother, Anna Bathory, was connected to the royal family. With noble blood running through her veins, Elizabeth's future seemed secure and full of promise.

Growing up in the grand castles of her family, Elizabeth's childhood was one of comfort, but it was also marked by a shadow of violence. In the harsh world of feudal Hungary, punishments for disobedience among the servants were severe, often brutal. Elizabeth witnessed these punishments firsthand, and some say that these early experiences shaped her later behavior. Despite her young age, she was known to be intelligent and strong-willed, with a sharp mind that set her apart from her peers.

Her education was fitting for a noblewoman of her status. Elizabeth was taught multiple languages, including Latin, Greek, and German. She learned to read and write in Hungarian, a skill rare for women of the time. But beyond literature and music, her education also included lessons in managing large estates and overseeing servants—a role she would fully assume later in life.

Her family was large, but little is known about her relationships with her siblings. What is clear, however, is that her parents were strict, demanding, and often distant. Like most noble families, there was little affection in the household, and the pressures of status and discipline were ever-present.

At the age of 15, Elizabeth was married to Ferenc Nádasdy, a union arranged to solidify political alliances between two noble families. Ferenc, known as "The Black Knight" for his ruthless prowess on the battlefield, was a respected Hungarian nobleman and warrior. Their marriage, while arranged, was stable enough by the standards of the time. They had four children together, but with Ferenc frequently away on military campaigns, much of the responsibility for managing the estates fell on Elizabeth's shoulders.

It was during these years, alone and burdened with the control of vast lands and hundreds of servants, that rumors of Elizabeth's cruelty began to surface. Her reputation for harsh discipline preceded her. Stories spread of young servant girls who would mysteriously disappear after being sent to work in her castles, though few dared to openly challenge a noblewoman of her stature.

The death of her husband in 1604 marked a turning point in Elizabeth's life. With Ferenc gone, Elizabeth was left to manage their estates on her own. The responsibilities weighed heavily on her, but she handled them with an iron fist. She ruled with absolute authority, but her behavior grew increasingly erratic and cruel. Dark rumors began to swirl—that the Countess was not only cruel to her servants but was responsible for their deaths. It was whispered that she had developed a macabre obsession with youth and beauty.

As the legend goes, Elizabeth Bathory believed that bathing in the blood of young girls would keep her eternally youthful. Whether these stories are true or the product of myth, the rumors were enough to fuel fear and suspicion. Victims were often peasant girls sent to work in her castle. According to witnesses, Elizabeth tortured them—using whips, knives, and other devices—before killing them. Some accounts describe the Countess watching her victims bleed, fascinated by their pain.

For years, Elizabeth continued her reign of terror, protected by her noble status. Even as the rumors intensified, few were willing to openly accuse a woman of such power. But her cruelty could not remain hidden forever. In 1610, after the disappearance of a noble-born girl who had been sent to her castle, the complaints of the local villagers grew louder. It was no longer just whispers among the peasants; it had become a scandal that the Hungarian court could not ignore.

King Matthias II of Hungary ordered an investigation. Led by György Thurzó, a powerful Hungarian noble and distant relative of the Countess, the investigation uncovered evidence of Elizabeth's atrocities. When Thurzó and his men entered her castle, they were said to have found a scene of horror—dead and dying girls, some barely clinging to life, their bodies mutilated and bloodied.

Elizabeth Bathory was arrested, and a sensational trial followed. The testimonies of witnesses were harrowing, recounting tales of torture that shocked the Hungarian court. Servants of the Countess, some of whom had been complicit in her crimes, were also arrested and put on trial. Under torture, they confessed to assisting Elizabeth in her gruesome deeds. They were executed for their roles in the murders, but the Countess's noble status spared her from the same fate.

Instead of execution, Elizabeth was sentenced to life imprisonment. She was confined to a small, windowless room in her castle, where she spent the last four years of her life. No one knows exactly what her final days were like, but it is said that she remained unrepentant until the end. On August 21, 1614, Elizabeth Bathory was found dead in her cell. She was 54 years old.

The number of her victims is still debated. Some sources claim she killed as many as 600 girls, while others put the number closer to 80. Regardless of the exact figure, her crimes were unprecedented in their brutality, and her name became synonymous with evil.

Elizabeth's story did not die with her. Over the centuries, she has become a figure of legend—a symbol of female cruelty, power, and unchecked ambition. Her alleged crimes have inspired countless books, films, and even plays, with some portraying her as a vampire-like figure who bathed in the blood of virgins to retain her youth. Whether these stories are based on truth or have been exaggerated over time is still a matter of debate among historians. Some argue that Elizabeth Bathory was the victim of a conspiracy, her powerful family enemies seeking to bring her down. Others believe that the evidence against her, gathered during the trial, speaks for itself.

Today, Elizabeth Bathory is remembered as one of the most infamous female serial killers in history. Her life and alleged crimes serve as a chilling reminder of the potential for cruelty, especially when power goes unchecked. The Countess, once a symbol of noble status and privilege, became a symbol of the darkest aspects of human nature.

Her legacy continues to fascinate, not only because of the sheer horror of her alleged crimes but because of the questions they raise about power, responsibility, and justice. Was she truly the monster history has painted her as, or was she the victim of a political vendetta? We may never know the full truth of Elizabeth Bathory's life, but her name will forever be etched in the annals of history as the Blood Countess.

18. The Vampire of Barcelona

E nriqueta Martí, known as the "Vampire of Barcelona," is one of Spain's most chilling and notorious criminals. Her life, born out of poverty and desperation, became a terrifying tale of kidnapping, murder, and dark practices that left the city of Barcelona in shock. Her crimes have etched her name in history, symbolizing the darkest depths of human nature.

Enriqueta Martí was born on February 2, 1868, in San Feliu de Llobregat, a small town near Barcelona. It was a bitterly cold winter's day, and Enriqueta came into the world as the daughter of poor peasants. Her father, a laborer, and her mother, a homemaker, struggled to provide for their family. The hardships of daily life were constant companions for Enriqueta, whose childhood was marked by poverty, hunger, and a growing sense of desperation.

Growing up in a cramped and modest home, the young Enriqueta was exposed to the harsh realities of life early on. She was expected to contribute to the household from a young age, leaving school early to help with chores and take on odd jobs. Her lack of formal education limited her options and fueled her bitterness. In a world where opportunities were scarce, Enriqueta was determined to survive by any means necessary.

Her family's financial difficulties created tension in the household. With several siblings, all competing for attention and resources, Enriqueta's childhood was far from nurturing. Her parents did their best, but the constant struggle to make ends meet took a toll on everyone.

Enriqueta married twice in her life. Her first marriage ended in divorce—a rare occurrence at the time, hinting at the turbulence in her relationships. Her second marriage was no more successful, and after the death of her only son at a young age, Enriqueta's fragile mental state seemed to unravel completely. The loss deepened her despair and set her on a dark path that would lead her to infamy.

One of Enriqueta's early passions was herbal medicine. She claimed to possess knowledge of traditional remedies and began selling potions and cures to those in need. In the poor neighborhoods of Barcelona, where medical care was scarce, people often turned to healers like Enriqueta in their desperation.

But her interest in healing soon became overshadowed by a more sinister fascination with the occult.

Enriqueta's life took a grim turn as she began delving deeper into crime. At first, she engaged in petty theft and fraud, using her herbal remedies as a front to con her way into people's trust. As her desperation for money and power grew, so did the scale of her crimes. She began kidnapping children, luring them away from the streets of Barcelona with promises of food or work.

What started as abductions soon escalated into something far more horrifying. Enriqueta was accused of murdering her young victims and using their remains in dark rituals. She believed that children's blood and body parts could be used to create powerful potions and cures, which she sold to wealthy clients who sought healing or rejuvenation. Her knowledge of herbs, combined with her twisted practices, allowed her to evade suspicion for years.

For a long time, Enriqueta's crimes went unnoticed. She moved through Barcelona's streets, blending into the shadows and taking children from the poorest neighborhoods, where they were least likely to be missed. The city, in the early 20th century, was a bustling, chaotic place, filled with both extreme wealth and poverty. In the poorer districts, the lives of children were often precarious. Enriqueta exploited this vulnerability to satisfy her gruesome needs.

In 1912, Enriqueta's crimes were finally exposed, but not before she had left a trail of horror in her wake. The police raided her home and made a discovery that would shock the entire nation. Inside, they found children's clothing, bones, bloodstained tools, and a list of wealthy clients who had purchased her potions. The scene was grotesque, and the sheer scale of her depravity sent shockwaves through Barcelona.

Enriqueta Martí was arrested, and the subsequent trial was one of the most sensational in Spanish history. The public was horrified to learn of the details of her crimes. How could a seemingly ordinary woman, posing as a healer and a helper of the poor, have committed such atrocities? During her trial, Enriqueta showed no remorse. She denied the charges against her, insisting that she had done nothing wrong. But the evidence was overwhelming, and the testimonies of witnesses painted a terrifying picture of her dark deeds.

Enriqueta's mental state was a subject of much debate. Was she driven to madness by her desperate circumstances, or had she always harbored a darker, more malevolent nature? Some believed that her fascination with the occult had clouded her judgment, turning her into a remorseless killer. Others thought that her crimes were born out of pure greed and the need for power.

Her downfall came swiftly after the trial. Though sentenced to life imprisonment, Enriqueta did not live long enough to serve her full sentence. She died under mysterious circumstances in prison, possibly murdered by fellow inmates who were disgusted by her crimes. Her death brought an end to the reign of terror she had inflicted on Barcelona, but the scars of her actions remained.

Enriqueta Martí's legacy is one of horror and caution. Her crimes raised awareness about the dangers faced by vulnerable children in the chaotic urban sprawl of early 20th-century Barcelona. The revelations of her actions led to calls for reforms in child protection and greater efforts to monitor the city's poorest neighborhoods.

While many saw her as a symbol of pure evil, some also viewed her story as a reflection of the deep inequalities and social problems of the time. The desperate poverty that drove her to crime was, in many ways, a product of the harsh conditions in which she lived. Enriqueta became a reminder of how easily the vulnerable could be exploited in a world that offered them little protection.

Today, Enriqueta Martí's name still resonates in Spain, her story a dark chapter in the country's history. Her life and crimes have inspired numerous works of fiction, from horror novels to films, each exploring the macabre details of her twisted actions. The legend of the "Vampire of Barcelona" has taken on a life of its own, blending fact and fiction into a chilling tale that continues to captivate and horrify.

In the end, Enriqueta's story is a tragic reminder of the depths of human cruelty and the importance of safeguarding society's most vulnerable. Her ability to deceive and manipulate those around her, hiding her monstrous nature behind the facade of a healer, makes her one of history's most terrifying figures.

19. The Tragic Descent

F rancisca Ballesteros, a name that once meant nothing more than an ordinary woman in a quiet Spanish town, now carries the weight of horror and betrayal. Behind her seemingly normal life as a wife and mother, lurked a deep darkness that eventually led her to commit unthinkable crimes. The early 2000s would forever mark her as one of Spain's most infamous female serial killers. Francisca's story is one of quiet despair, deep mental conflict, and the ultimate unraveling of a woman who felt trapped in her life.

Born on May 21, 1969, in Valencia, Spain, Francisca entered the world on a bright spring day in a bustling Mediterranean city. Her parents were simple working-class people who tried to provide a decent life for their children. Her father was a laborer, and her mother took care of the home. Life was modest, and though her parents worked hard, financial struggles were a constant presence. For young Francisca, the environment felt suffocating, and she often found herself retreating into solitude.

Francisca's childhood wasn't filled with the warmth and joy many expect from early family life. She was distant and introverted, preferring her own company over playing with other children. As she grew, her emotional isolation deepened. Though she attended local schools in Valencia, she was an average student and showed no particular interest in her studies. By the time she finished high school, she had already abandoned any dreams of higher education. She left school to help support her family, a decision that would later haunt her as she felt increasingly trapped in the life she had never wanted.

Her family, though hardworking, was often emotionally absent. Francisca's relationships with her siblings were strained, as her preference for isolation meant that she rarely engaged with them in a meaningful way. The family dynamic was one of financial stress and emotional distance, further pushing Francisca into a world of her own thoughts and feelings, disconnected from the world around her.

In her early twenties, Francisca sought an escape from her home life and married Antonio González Barribino. At first glance, they seemed like a typical Spanish couple, settling into their married life in Valencia and raising three children: a daughter, Florinda, and two sons, Antonio and José. But beneath the surface, their marriage was far from idyllic. Antonio worked long hours, and the strain of financial instability weighed heavily on the couple. Francisca found herself overwhelmed by the demands of motherhood and the never-ending grind of domestic life. She had little time for herself and felt trapped by her responsibilities.

Francisca had few hobbies, and the little time she had for herself was spent watching television or reading. But these small pleasures did nothing to alleviate the growing sense of emptiness that gnawed at her. She longed for something more but saw no way out of her life. Her marriage, which should have been a source of partnership and support, became another source of stress. Antonio, her husband, was often distant, and the love that once existed between them faded as the pressures of life mounted.

Over time, Francisca's mental state began to deteriorate. She felt as though her life was spiraling out of control. Trapped in a loveless marriage and burdened with financial difficulties, she saw no escape. The once quiet and introverted woman became consumed by a sense of hopelessness. There was no joy in her daily routine, only a growing resentment toward the family she felt shackled her to a life she didn't want.

In 2004, Francisca made a decision that would forever change the course of her life. She began plotting to murder her family. The plan seemed unfathomable—a mother methodically planning the deaths of her children and husband, the very people she was meant to love and protect. But in her mind, this was the only way out. She convinced herself that by killing them, she could finally escape the life that had trapped her.

In January of that year, Francisca's plan began. Her first target was her 15-year-old daughter, Florinda. On a seemingly normal day, Francisca prepared a lethal dose of sleeping pills and administered it to her daughter, who died quietly in her sleep. The family believed Florinda's death was the result of natural causes, and Francisca continued her life as though nothing had happened. But inside, she was preparing for the next step.

The death of her daughter didn't provide the relief Francisca had hoped for. Instead, her despair deepened, and her next target became her husband, Antonio. In June of 2004, she attempted to poison him, but her plan failed—he survived the initial attempt. Undeterred, she tried again later that year in

December, and this time, she succeeded. Antonio died, and once again, Francisca acted as though it had been an unfortunate accident.

Her final victim was her son, Antonio. In January 2005, she tried to poison him, but this time, her plan unraveled. Her son fell seriously ill, and doctors grew suspicious of the symptoms. Investigations soon revealed the truth—Francisca had been systematically poisoning her family. She was arrested, and the gruesome details of her crimes shocked the nation.

Francisca Ballesteros, once a quiet homemaker, was now one of Spain's most notorious criminals. The trial that followed was a media sensation. The public couldn't understand how a mother could commit such horrific acts against her own children. What drove her to kill those she should have loved and protected? Francisca showed little remorse during the trial, and the courtroom was filled with tension as she recounted her crimes.

Mental health experts debated her state of mind. Some believed she had suffered a mental breakdown brought on by years of emotional isolation, financial stress, and a loveless marriage. Others saw her actions as cold, calculated, and unforgivable. The truth likely lay somewhere in between—a desperate woman, trapped in her own mind, who saw murder as her only escape.

Francisca was sentenced to life in prison, where she remains today. Her story continues to haunt Spain, a chilling reminder of the potential for violence hidden within seemingly ordinary lives. Her case has prompted discussions about mental health, particularly the need for better support systems for those who feel isolated and overwhelmed by life's pressures.

Her legacy is a dark one. Francisca Ballesteros's name is now synonymous with betrayal, the ultimate breach of trust. Her actions left a deep scar on Spanish society, serving as a grim reminder that sometimes the greatest dangers come from within the family unit.

20. The Chilling Case of Horror

Genene Jones, a name that now evokes fear and horror across the United States, is infamous for her heinous crimes as a pediatric nurse. Between the late 1970s and early 1980s, she was responsible for the deaths of numerous infants and children under her care, making her one of the most disturbing figures in medical history. Her actions shocked the nation, revealing the terrifying potential for abuse of trust within the healthcare system and leading to critical changes in hospital protocols.

Born on July 13, 1950, in Texas, Genene Jones entered a world of heat and humidity typical of the state. She was adopted shortly after birth by a couple who already had three biological sons. Her adoptive father owned a nightclub, while her mother was a homemaker. Though they provided for her materially, Genene's emotional needs were often left unmet. She felt overshadowed by her older brothers, sparking a lifelong need for attention and validation.

Genene's childhood was defined by isolation. While her family cared for her physical needs, they struggled to connect with her emotionally. Her brothers seemed to outshine her in every way, leaving Genene desperate for acknowledgment. This emotional gap left her yearning for love and approval, feelings that would later twist into something far darker.

In school, Genene was an average student. She wasn't known for excelling academically, but she did display a growing interest in nursing and caring for others. After high school, she enrolled in a vocational nursing program, a choice that seemed to align with her desire to be needed. Yet, beneath the surface of her caring exterior, Genene harbored darker intentions.

Her relationships were equally troubled. In her early twenties, Genene married James "Jimmy" Harvey DeLany, but the marriage quickly deteriorated, ending in divorce after just a few years. Her second marriage was no better. By 1977, she had given birth to her only child, Richard, but motherhood didn't bring her the fulfillment she had longed for. Instead, her emotional instability deepened, and she sought out other means to gain the attention she craved.

Her nursing career became her primary focus. Genene quickly earned a reputation for her dedication, particularly in pediatric care. She seemed to thrive in moments of crisis, often volunteering for extra shifts and emergencies.

Colleagues initially admired her, describing her as the nurse who was always there in the worst moments, ready to help. "She was caring, or so we thought," one nurse recalled. "Always willing to step in when a child was in trouble." But in hindsight, Genene's presence in those critical moments was no coincidence.

In 1981, Genene began working at Bexar County Medical Center in San Antonio, Texas, a place where her dark side would fully emerge. Here, she had access to vulnerable children and the medications that would soon become her instruments of terror. The pediatric unit became her hunting ground. Genene administered lethal doses of drugs like digoxin, heparin, and succinylcholine to young patients, causing medical crises that she could then attempt to "fix." For a time, her actions made her appear heroic—a nurse who could bring children back from the brink of death. But her need for recognition came at the cost of innocent lives.

Genene's method was both cunning and chilling. She would administer just enough of the drug to send a child into distress, setting the stage for a dramatic emergency that she could swoop in to manage. If the child survived, she appeared to be a hero. If they died, she was often able to avoid suspicion, as infant deaths in intensive care units were not uncommon. The thrill of being in control, of holding life and death in her hands, seemed to consume her. She basked in the praise and attention she received, but behind the façade, the body count was growing.

Her first known victim was Chelsea McClellan, a 15-month-old girl who died under Genene's care in 1982. Chelsea had been admitted for minor health issues, but after Genene administered a fatal dose of succinylcholine, a muscle relaxant, Chelsea went into cardiac arrest and died. It was a tragedy that rocked the family but didn't raise immediate suspicions. To the McClellans, Genene was just the nurse who had tried to save their daughter.

As the months passed, more children died mysteriously at Bexar County Medical Center. Genene was often the nurse on duty during these deaths, but it wasn't until a few brave doctors and nurses began noticing patterns in her behavior that an investigation was launched. By then, the damage had been done. Too many children had lost their lives under Genene's care, and their families were left shattered, unaware of the true cause of their heartbreak.

In 1983, suspicions finally caught up with Genene. An internal investigation into the unusually high number of pediatric deaths at the hospital pointed to her involvement. She had managed to evade scrutiny for so long because of the chaotic nature of pediatric ICU work, where children's health could deteriorate rapidly and without warning. But as evidence mounted, the truth became undeniable.

Genene Jones was arrested in 1984 and charged with the murder of Chelsea McClellan, as well as the attempted murder of 4-week-old Rolando Santos. During her trial, she maintained her innocence, insisting that she had only ever wanted to help the children in her care. "I never intended to hurt anyone. I just wanted to be needed," she claimed. Her cold and calculated behavior during the trial shocked the public. She showed no remorse, even as the evidence piled up against her.

Colleagues who had once admired her were horrified. "We trusted her with our most vulnerable patients," one doctor said in disbelief. "None of us could have imagined that she was the one behind it all."

In 1985, Genene was convicted of murder and injury to a child. She was sentenced to 99 years in prison for the murder of Chelsea McClellan and 60 years for the injury of Rolando Santos. Her arrest and conviction sent shockwaves through the medical community, highlighting the terrifying potential for abuse of power within the healthcare system. Her case led to immediate changes in hospital protocols, particularly in the handling and administration of medications. Hospitals across the country implemented stricter oversight of patient care and drug administration to prevent another tragedy like the one Genene had caused.

Genene's actions had lasting consequences, not only for the families of her victims but also for the medical profession as a whole. Her crimes exposed critical flaws in the healthcare system, where a single nurse could go unchecked for so long. In the years following her conviction, hospitals introduced reforms aimed at improving patient safety, ensuring that no healthcare professional could wield such unchecked power over life and death again.

Today, Genene Jones remains a symbol of the darkest side of the medical profession. Her story is a chilling reminder that even those entrusted with the care of society's most vulnerable can become predators. Her need for attention and validation drove her to commit unimaginable acts, leaving a trail of grief and heartbreak in her wake. Her legacy is one of caution—a warning that trust, once broken, can have deadly consequences.

The tale of Genene Jones will forever be etched in the annals of criminal history. Her betrayal of trust, her cold manipulation, and her willingness to kill for recognition make her one of the most infamous serial killers in American history.

21. The Walking Death

G esche Gottfried was born on March 6, 1785, in Bremen, Germany. She came from a modest background, her father was a hardworking tailor and her mother was a strict homemaker. Bremen's spring weather was chilly, and her early life reflected the harsh conditions of lower-middle-class life. Her upbringing taught her the value of hard work and obedience, but also left her with a desire for something more—a life of comfort and stability that always seemed just out of reach. These early struggles would shape her into one of history's most notorious female serial killers.

Gesche's childhood was not filled with warmth. Her relationship with her parents was strained, particularly with her mother, who was cold and demanding. Her father, though kinder, was often preoccupied with his work. Gesche had siblings, but the bond with them was distant. The one person she truly cared for was her brother, Johann, who later, tragically, became one of her victims. This difficult family life contributed to the internal turmoil that would later drive her to commit unthinkable acts.

In 1806, at the age of 21, Gesche married Johann Mittenberg, a wealthy merchant who provided the financial stability she longed for. They had three children—two sons, Johann and Heinrich, and a daughter, Adelheid. On the surface, the marriage brought her a comfortable life, but it was far from happy. Johann was frequently away on business, leaving Gesche alone with her children, isolated and unfulfilled. Despite the wealth, something inside Gesche began to twist.

Her interests were focused on her family and household. She took pride in her domestic skills—cooking, cleaning, and caring for the children. But behind this facade of a devoted wife and mother, a deep dissatisfaction grew. She wanted more than just managing a household. She craved control, wealth, and independence, and this desire would soon drive her to take matters into her own hands in the most horrific way.

Her first murder came in 1813 when she decided to poison her husband, Johann. Using arsenic, a deadly poison, she carefully administered it in small doses over time. His illness seemed to worsen naturally, and when he finally died, no one suspected foul play. She gained sympathy from friends and neighbors for her "loss" and inherited money from Johann's estate. It was the first step toward her darker path.

Gesche's mind was already corrupted by this sense of empowerment. The ability to end a life without suspicion filled her with a twisted sense of control. She saw death not as a tragedy but as a means to an end. And so, she continued. Her own children became her next victims. One by one, she poisoned them, taking care to appear as the grieving mother to her community. People pitied her; they never imagined that the woman who seemed so caring could be responsible for such horrors.

Gesche's ability to deceive those around her was remarkable. Despite the growing number of deaths surrounding her, no one suspected her. She was kind, gentle, and always willing to help care for the sick. People began to call her the "Angel of Bremen," believing she had a gift for comforting the dying. But in truth, she was the very cause of their deaths. She found a twisted pleasure in watching her victims suffer slowly, their lives slipping away at her hands.

After her family was gone, Gesche didn't stop. She turned to her friends and neighbors. Her brother Johann, her parents, and several close friends all fell victim to her deadly plans. Each death brought her more sympathy, sometimes money, and always the sense of control she craved. She had mastered the art of slow poisoning, using arsenic to induce long, drawn-out illnesses. As they withered away, she was by their side, offering false comfort while secretly sealing their fate.

In the community, she was loved and admired. She kept up the appearance of a heartbroken woman who had lost everyone dear to her. People trusted her with their lives, never knowing that they were walking into the hands of a killer. Her house became a place of death, yet no one suspected a thing. It was a horrifying game for Gesche, and she played it with cold precision.

But in 1828, her luck ran out. After the death of her last victim, rumors began to spread. The sheer number of deaths surrounding her life could no longer be ignored. Suspicion crept into the minds of those around her. People who had once admired her began to whisper, and the authorities took notice. An investigation was launched, and when the bodies of her victims were exhumed, traces of arsenic were found in their remains.

Gesche was arrested, and the community that once called her an angel now turned on her. At her trial, she remained cold and detached. The woman who had once seemed so kind and caring showed no remorse for the lives she had taken. Her meticulous notes detailing the doses of poison she had administered to her victims were presented as evidence, revealing a calculated and ruthless murderer. The public was horrified by the revelations. How could someone so trusted have committed such atrocities?

Gesche was sentenced to death, and on April 21, 1831, she was publicly executed by beheading. It was a day of grim satisfaction for the people of Bremen. As they watched her execution, they knew that justice had been served. But the legacy of her crimes would linger long after her death. The "Angel of Bremen" had betrayed the trust of an entire community, and her story became a cautionary tale, a dark reminder that evil can hide behind the most innocent of faces.

Gesche Gottfried's life was a chilling example of how a desire for control and financial security can drive a person to commit unspeakable acts. Her ability to deceive and manipulate those around her allowed her to carry out her crimes for years without detection. But in the end, her greed and cruelty were her undoing.

Her story left a profound impact on society, particularly in Bremen, where her crimes prompted significant changes in the way suspicious deaths were investigated. The forensic science of the time began to develop more rigorous methods for detecting poisoning, and the case became a landmark in the history of criminal investigations in Germany.

Today, Gesche Gottfried is remembered as one of Germany's most notorious female serial killers. Her crimes serve as a dark chapter in history, a reminder of the dangers of unchecked trust and the potential for evil within those who seem the most innocent. Her legacy is one of horror, but also the importance of vigilance and the need for justice in the face of unimaginable betrayal.

22. The Poisoner's Legacy

Giulia Tofana, a name that conjures fear and intrigue, was one of the most notorious figures of 17th-century Italy. Known for her lethal invention, Aqua Tofana, Giulia provided desperate women with a means to escape abusive marriages through the dark art of poisoning. Her story is one of desperation, innovation, and betrayal, leaving a lasting mark on history with an estimated 600 victims attributed to her infamous poison.

Born around 1620 in Palermo, Italy, Giulia's early life was shaped by the Mediterranean climate and the turbulent social realities of the time. Her mother, Thofania d'Adamo, was a poisoner who was executed for her crimes in 1633. Little is known about Giulia's father, who is believed to have died early in her life. The young Giulia grew up in an atmosphere thick with secrecy, fear, and a shadow of guilt from her mother's criminal past. From an early age, she was exposed to poisons, learning about herbs and toxic substances, which would later become her deadly tools.

The streets of Palermo during her childhood were bustling with life. Vendors, merchants, and sailors filled the narrow cobbled roads, but Giulia lived in a different world—one shrouded in the knowledge of life and death through unnatural means. Her education was minimal, focused on domestic skills as was expected for girls of her time, but she was particularly adept in herbalism and remedies, skills she learned from her mother. It was this knowledge that would soon become her weapon.

Giulia married young, though the details of her husband are scarce. What is known is that her marriage, like so many in her era, was likely oppressive and unhappy. She had a daughter, Girolama Spera, who would eventually follow in her footsteps. Giulia's position as a woman in a patriarchal society left her with few options. The legal system did little to protect women, especially in cases of domestic abuse, and divorce was unthinkable. Women trapped in abusive marriages had no escape—except for death, and Giulia would offer them that route.

In the early years of her criminal career, Giulia lived a double life. To the public, she was a humble woman who made beauty products and remedies. But in private, she was becoming the mastermind behind one of the deadliest poison rings in history. Her invention, Aqua Tofana, was a colorless, tasteless poison made from a mixture of arsenic, lead, and belladonna. It was sold disguised as a cosmetic product, specifically a facial oil or holy water, making it easy for women to administer it without raising suspicion.

The poison worked slowly, often mimicking natural illness, allowing the victim's death to seem unremarkable. The brilliance of Aqua Tofana lay in its subtlety. A few drops in food or drink were administered over time, and the victim would fall ill, eventually dying without anyone suspecting foul play. Giulia's clients, often desperate women trapped in loveless or violent marriages, would visit her in secret. She provided them not only with the poison but also with detailed instructions on how to use it without arousing suspicion. It was crucial to administer the poison gradually, she would say, ensuring that the husband's death would seem natural.

The women who came to her were from all walks of life—some wealthy, others poor—but all shared a sense of entrapment. Giulia became known as a savior among them, offering them the only escape they could see from their unbearable lives. Her reputation spread through whispers, and soon, she had an extensive network of clients throughout Rome, Naples, and beyond.

For years, Giulia's poison ring operated in the shadows, evading detection. The death toll continued to rise, but the authorities remained unaware. To the women she helped, Giulia was a saint, providing them with freedom at a time when society offered them none. To others, she was a deadly criminal hiding behind a facade of kindness.

The turning point in Giulia's life came in 1659 when a woman who had purchased Aqua Tofana for her husband had second thoughts. Consumed with guilt and fear, the woman confessed her plan to a priest, who immediately reported it to the authorities. This confession sparked an investigation that led to Giulia's arrest. When the authorities raided her home, they found vials of Aqua Tofana, disguised as beauty products, and detailed records of her sales.

Under torture, Giulia confessed to her crimes. She revealed that she had been supplying poison to women for decades, leading to the deaths of over 600 men. Her calm and collected demeanor during the confession stunned her interrogators. She did not see herself as a villain but as a savior, offering desperate women a way out of their suffering. "I only gave them what they needed," she reportedly said.

Giulia, along with her daughter Girolama and several accomplices, was executed in Rome in 1659. Her death marked the end of one of the most notorious poisoning rings in history, but her legacy lived on. The fear of poison lingered in Italy long after her execution, and her story became a legend, passed down through generations as a cautionary tale.

The impact of Giulia's actions extended beyond the hundreds of deaths she caused. Her case highlighted the desperation of women in oppressive marriages, shedding light on the lack of legal recourse available to them. It also led to greater awareness of the dangers of poison and prompted changes in how suspicious deaths were investigated. Forensic science began to evolve, with more attention given to the possibility of poisoning in cases of sudden or unexplained deaths.

Giulia's life was a paradox. To some, she was a hero, a woman who empowered others to take control of their lives in the only way available to them. To others, she was a cold-blooded murderer who took advantage of vulnerable women and left a trail of death in her wake. Her story remains a complex one, blending elements of heroism, villainy, and the harsh realities of life in 17th-century Italy.

Today, Giulia Tofana is remembered as both a criminal mastermind and a symbol of desperation. Her invention of Aqua Tofana was an act of ingenuity, but the lives it claimed cannot be ignored. Her legacy is a dark reminder of the lengths people will go to when they feel trapped, and how society can fail its most vulnerable members.

In the end, Giulia's story is one of survival, both for herself and for the women she helped. It's a tale of the human capacity for both compassion and cruelty, wrapped in the guise of beauty and death.

23. Lethal Lovers' Dark Deeds

Gwendolyn Graham and Cathy Wood, two women who seemed to blend into the quiet backdrop of caregiving, would forever change the landscape of elder care in America. Their crimes, committed under the guise of compassion and care, shocked the nation in the late 1980s. These were not just isolated incidents of neglect or malice; Gwendolyn and Cathy had formed a deadly bond, using murder as a twisted way to solidify their relationship.

Gwendolyn Graham was born on August 6, 1963, in Santa Fe, New Mexico, a city surrounded by desert heat and mountain skies. Her childhood was marked by instability. Allegations of abuse and neglect from her father set the stage for her psychological turbulence. Gwendolyn learned early on how to distance herself emotionally from the chaos around her, a skill that would serve her well later in life when her crimes required cold detachment. She moved frequently, making it difficult to form stable friendships, and carried the scars of an abusive upbringing.

Cathy Wood, born on March 7, 1962, in Toledo, Ohio, had a childhood that looked different from Gwendolyn's on the surface but was equally lonely. She grew up feeling neglected by her parents, though her life wasn't marked by the same turbulence that shaped Gwendolyn's early years. Cathy often retreated into herself, becoming reserved and harboring feelings of inadequacy. This emotional detachment would later manifest in darker ways as she sought validation from her partner, Gwendolyn.

Neither woman excelled in school, and both finished high school without much direction. Cathy married young and had a daughter, but her marriage was strained and filled with emotional neglect. She craved attention and love but felt invisible within her own family. Gwendolyn, on the other hand, avoided marriage and motherhood altogether, preferring to maintain control over her life without the bonds of traditional family expectations. When the two women met while working as nurse's aides at Alpine Manor in Walker, Michigan, their lives would collide in a way no one could have predicted.

Alpine Manor was supposed to be a place of care and comfort for the elderly, many of whom were unable to care for themselves. The atmosphere was quiet, the halls filled with the low hum of medical machines and the occasional chatter of residents and staff. It was a world of routine, and yet, within this seemingly serene environment, Gwendolyn and Cathy found a perverse way to bond. What began as a romantic relationship soon spiraled into something much darker.

Gwendolyn and Cathy bonded over a shared sense of mischief and control, which began to manifest in chilling ways. They developed a private game, a secret ritual that involved suffocating their elderly patients. To them, it was a twisted form of intimacy, a shared secret that solidified their relationship. Gwendolyn, often the instigator, would smother the victims with washcloths, while Cathy watched or assisted. The thrill of control over life and death became an obsession, and with each murder, their bond grew stronger.

The elderly women they chose were vulnerable, often confused, and helpless. Gwendolyn and Cathy selected their victims carefully—those who wouldn't be missed or whose deaths would seem natural. The victims' final moments were filled with terror, but their cries went unheard. Afterward, Gwendolyn and Cathy would reflect on their acts with a sense of pride, treating the murders as their own morbid love notes to one another.

"It's like we're playing God," Gwendolyn once whispered to Cathy after one of their kills. Cathy would later recall this moment in court, a haunting reminder of the depth of their depravity. What made their crimes even more chilling was the complete lack of remorse they showed. They saw their actions as a way to strengthen their relationship, not as the murders they truly were.

At first, no one suspected anything unusual. In a nursing home, deaths are not uncommon, and many of the victims were elderly women who had been ill for some time. But Gwendolyn and Cathy weren't careful enough. Their playful attitude towards death, and their mocking of their victims after their murders, began to raise suspicion among their coworkers. It wasn't just the frequency of the deaths but also how the women behaved afterward. It seemed like every time Gwendolyn and Cathy were on shift together, another patient mysteriously died.

Tension grew between the two women as well. Cathy, always the more passive one, began to feel trapped. Gwendolyn's control over her became suffocating, and Cathy's fear of being caught grew with each death. Their relationship, once built on excitement and shared secrets, started to fray. Cathy began to question Gwendolyn's growing obsession with death, but by then, they were both in too deep.

In the spring of 1988, Cathy finally broke. Overwhelmed by guilt and fear, she confessed to her ex-husband, who immediately went to the police. Cathy, in an attempt to save herself from the full brunt of justice, painted Gwendolyn as the mastermind behind the killings. She claimed she had been manipulated, that she was afraid of Gwendolyn and had no choice but to go along with the murders. In reality, the truth was more complicated. Cathy had been a willing participant, but she saw her opportunity to shift the blame and took it.

When the police arrested Gwendolyn, she was calm, almost indifferent. She denied the accusations at first, but Cathy's testimony sealed her fate. The investigation revealed that at least five elderly women had been murdered, though the true number might have been higher. Gwendolyn was sentenced to life in prison without the possibility of parole, while Cathy received a lighter sentence in exchange for her cooperation.

In court, Cathy showed no remorse. "It was fun to kill," she said chillingly, her words sending shockwaves through the courtroom. Gwendolyn remained silent for most of the trial, her cold demeanor in stark contrast to the horror of her actions. The case drew national attention, with many questioning how two caregivers, trusted with the lives of the most vulnerable, could turn into cold-blooded killers.

The impact of their crimes reverberated beyond the nursing home. The case prompted sweeping changes in the elder care industry. Nursing homes faced increased scrutiny, with new regulations requiring more thorough background checks on employees and stricter oversight of staff behavior. The vulnerability of elderly patients, often forgotten and left in the care of strangers, became a national concern.

The legacy of Gwendolyn Graham and Cathy Wood is one of horror and betrayal. They took advantage of their positions as caregivers to commit unspeakable acts of cruelty. Their actions shattered the trust placed in those who care for the elderly and vulnerable, leaving a scar on the healthcare system that would take years to heal.

To this day, Gwendolyn remains in prison, serving her life sentence, while Cathy continues to insist that she was merely a pawn in Gwendolyn's deadly game. Their story is a reminder of the darkness that can lurk behind seemingly benign facades, and of the terrible consequences that can arise when power is abused. The Alpine Manor killings, driven by a twisted sense of love and control, serve as one of the most chilling examples of evil hiding in plain sight.

Their crimes continue to be studied by criminologists and psychologists, who examine the psychological dynamics of their relationship and the pathology of their actions. Gwendolyn and Cathy, once trusted caregivers, will forever be remembered as the "Lethal Lovers," their twisted bond sealed in blood.

24. The Poisonous Cook

Helene Jegado, a name now infamous in French criminal history, once seemed like an ordinary woman living a quiet life. Born on June 17, 1803, in the small village of Plouhinec, Brittany, her beginnings were simple. Brittany was a place of old traditions, where the ocean's breeze swept through the rural countryside, and the daily life of peasants was hard but predictable. Helene, the daughter of a weaver, was no stranger to this harsh life. Her early years were marked by the grind of poverty, an existence full of struggle and deprivation. It was here, in these modest surroundings, that the seeds of her dark future were planted.

Helene's childhood was a joyless one. The Jegado family lived in a small, rundown house, struggling to make ends meet. Her father was strict and often demanding, while her mother was distant, offering little affection or warmth. Helene was expected to help with household chores from a young age, and this constant burden left her feeling bitter and detached. Unlike other children who found solace in play, Helene seemed to retreat into herself, her coldness growing over the years. She had several siblings, but none of them were particularly close, and the family dynamic was tense and unforgiving.

With no formal education, Helene learned the basics of life through her mother—cooking, cleaning, and running a household. These domestic skills would later become the tools for her chilling crimes. By the time she reached adulthood, Helene found work as a domestic servant, moving from one household to another. In her role as a cook, she appeared competent and hardworking. But beneath this quiet demeanor was a woman capable of unfathomable cruelty.

Her early years as a servant were relatively unremarkable, and she quickly learned how to navigate the complexities of each household she worked for. She observed how power and control could shift within a family, and it fascinated her. The more she learned, the more she realized that, as a servant, she was invisible. Her employers rarely suspected that someone so ordinary could pose any threat. And so, she began to use this invisibility to her advantage.

In 1833, Helene committed her first known murder while working for the family of François Le Drogo. She poisoned one of her victims with arsenic, a substance that was easy to acquire in those days and difficult to detect. It was a slow, painful death, one that Helene watched unfold with an unsettling sense of calm. The victim's death was ruled as natural causes, and Helene was free to continue her work, now with the knowledge that she could kill without being caught.

Helene's preferred method was arsenic. It was a poison that left little trace, and when administered in small doses, it mimicked the symptoms of common illnesses like food poisoning or cholera. As she moved from household to household, Helene continued her deadly spree. She poisoned employers, their children, fellow servants—anyone who crossed her path. She would cook delicious meals, knowing that what she served was laced with death. Her victims would fall ill gradually, suffering before they eventually succumbed. And through it all, Helene remained composed, playing the part of the concerned servant while secretly enjoying the chaos she caused.

What drove Helene to commit such cold-blooded murders? Many believe it was a deep-seated need for control. As a woman in 19th-century France, her opportunities were limited, and her life as a servant was one of subjugation and invisibility. Poison became her way of asserting power in a world where she had none. By controlling life and death, she found a twisted sense of purpose and satisfaction. She could manipulate those who thought they were above her, all while maintaining her facade of humility.

Helene's murders were not motivated by greed or revenge. She rarely benefited financially from her victims' deaths. Instead, her actions appeared to be driven by a cold detachment, a lack of empathy that allowed her to view human life as expendable. The households she worked for trusted her implicitly, never suspecting that the quiet cook preparing their meals was responsible for the mysterious deaths occurring around them.

For nearly two decades, Helene's crimes went unnoticed. People died, and life went on. But her luck would not last forever. In 1851, after years of poisoning her victims without suspicion, Helene was finally arrested. By this time, rumors had begun to spread about the unusually high number of deaths that seemed to follow her from job to job. An investigation was launched, and arsenic was found in the bodies of several of her victims.

Her trial captivated the nation. The public was horrified to learn that someone so ordinary could be capable of such atrocities. In court, Helene showed no remorse. She sat stone-faced, listening to the testimonies of those who had known her, now shocked by her true nature. The quiet, unassuming servant they had trusted was revealed to be a monster in their midst.

During the trial, one former employer recalled how Helene had been praised for her cooking skills, unaware that those same meals had been the vehicle for murder. "She had a way with food," they said, "but we never suspected she had a way with poison as well." Helene remained emotionless, as though the events unfolding around her were of little consequence.

Despite her crimes, Helene Jegado maintained her innocence, claiming that she had done nothing wrong. But the evidence against her was overwhelming. The court found her guilty of multiple murders, and in 1852, she was executed by guillotine. Her death marked the end of one of France's most notorious serial killers, but the fear she had instilled lived on.

Helene Jegado's crimes left a lasting impact on French society. Her case brought to light the potential dangers lurking within the domestic sphere, where servants had unfettered access to the most intimate aspects of their employers' lives. It led to changes in how household staff were hired and monitored, with greater emphasis placed on background checks and oversight. No longer could families afford to take the trustworthiness of their servants for granted.

In the years that followed, Helene's story became a cautionary tale, a reminder of the darkness that can reside in even the most ordinary individuals. Her cold, methodical approach to murder and her ability to evade suspicion for so long shocked a society that had believed itself safe within the confines of the home.

Helene Jegado's legacy is one of fear and caution. She stands as a reminder that evil can hide behind the most mundane roles and that even a trusted cook can wield death with a calm, steady hand. Her story continues to fascinate and terrify, a testament to the chilling potential for cruelty that exists within the human soul. In the quiet kitchens of 19th-century France, Helene Jegado turned meals into instruments of death, and with each poisoned dish, she cemented her place in the annals of history as one of the most prolific female serial killers the world has ever known.

25. Satan in a Skirt

I rina Gaidamachuk's name evokes fear and disbelief in Russia. Known as the "Satan in a Skirt," she carried out a chilling series of murders that targeted elderly women in the early 2000s. What made her crimes even more horrifying was her ability to blend seamlessly into society, a seemingly normal woman living a quiet life, while beneath the surface lay a twisted and deadly mind.

Born on May 22, 1972, in the small town of Nyagan, in Russia's Khanty-Mansi Autonomous Okrug, Irina's childhood was far from ideal. Her family struggled with poverty, and her parents' battle with alcoholism made life chaotic and unstable. As a young girl, Irina often found herself in the role of a neglected child. Her parents, absorbed by their own problems, had little time for her, and this emotional void only grew as she matured.

Irina's education was basic. She attended the local school, but she was not particularly interested in academics. In the small town where she grew up, opportunities were limited, and it wasn't long before she realized that life offered her few paths to success. She became withdrawn, rarely connecting with her peers, and found solace in isolation.

Her family life was fragmented. Her relationship with her parents was strained due to their alcoholism, and although she had siblings, there was no strong bond between them. The lack of love and support during these formative years left Irina detached and cold. The cracks in her psyche began to form, though no one around her could have predicted the dark path she would later take.

In her early twenties, Irina married a man named Yuri Gaidamachuk. On the surface, it seemed like a fresh start for her, a chance to escape her difficult upbringing. Yuri was a hardworking man, but his own life was plagued by unemployment and financial instability. They had two children together, but their marriage quickly began to unravel. Yuri's struggles, combined with Irina's unresolved emotional turmoil, created a toxic environment at home. Irina began to spiral further into frustration and resentment. She lacked a sense of purpose and found herself overwhelmed by the weight of her mundane existence.

Irina showed little interest in hobbies or pursuits outside of her household duties. Her focus became centered on survival, on making ends meet, and soon, on something much darker. She had no positive role models or support system, and as her marriage faltered, Irina felt increasingly isolated. Her disillusionment with life began to harden into something more dangerous—a desire for control.

In 2002, her life took a disturbing turn when she committed her first murder. Her target was an elderly woman living in the Sverdlovsk Oblast region of Russia. Irina, posing as a social worker, gained the woman's trust before brutally killing her with a hammer. The brutality of the act shocked even Irina herself at first, but as the adrenaline faded, a sense of power took over. She had found something that gave her a twisted sense of control in her otherwise powerless life.

This first killing marked the beginning of a terrifying pattern. Over the next eight years, Irina continued to target elderly women, luring them into a false sense of security before taking their lives. She often posed as a social worker or someone in need, which allowed her to enter her victims' homes without raising suspicion. Her weapon of choice was always a hammer, and she attacked swiftly, leaving behind a gruesome scene of violence.

Her method was calculated and efficient. She struck hard and fast, taking what little valuables her victims had and leaving the crime scene as quietly as she had entered. The communities in Sverdlovsk were left reeling, not knowing that a serial killer was among them, walking the same streets, living the same quiet life as they were.

Her personal life, meanwhile, carried on as usual. At home, she was still the same Irina—quiet, withdrawn, a mother, and a wife. But beneath the facade, she was haunted by a growing sense of detachment. She continued to go unnoticed, blending into the fabric of society without arousing suspicion. Even her husband Yuri had no idea of the monster his wife had become. Irina's ability to carry out such heinous acts while maintaining her daily routines highlighted her chilling detachment from the value of human life.

Between 2002 and 2010, Irina murdered at least 17 elderly women. Her actions instilled fear and paranoia among the elderly population, especially in the small towns where her crimes took place. People began locking their doors, suspicious of anyone offering help. The elderly, once trusting and open, now lived in fear of strangers, unsure if they could even trust those they had once known.

But eventually, her luck ran out. In 2010, after nearly a decade of undetected killings, Irina was arrested. The investigation had been long and complicated, with police initially struggling to connect the murders. When they finally closed in on Irina, the truth of her crimes sent shockwaves through Russia. The woman who had once seemed so unassuming, so ordinary, had been hiding a monstrous secret.

Her trial was a spectacle. The media dubbed her "Satan in a Skirt," a reflection of the horror her crimes had evoked in the public. Irina herself, however, showed little emotion. During the trial, she remained cold and detached, offering no remorse for her actions. In the courtroom, her demeanor was unsettling—she appeared almost indifferent to the lives she had taken. When asked why she had committed the murders, Irina responded simply, "I needed the money."

It was a chilling statement, one that revealed the depths of her detachment and lack of empathy. She had viewed her victims not as people, but as means to an end, tools to satisfy her desire for financial gain and control.

The families of her victims were left devastated. Their loved ones had been targeted in their own homes, places they had once felt safe. The grief and anger in the courtroom were palpable, but Irina remained unmoved.

In the end, Irina Gaidamachuk was sentenced to 20 years in prison for her crimes. While justice had been served, the scars she left behind in the community would never fully heal. Her cold-blooded murders exposed the vulnerability of the elderly population and prompted changes in how social workers and caregivers were monitored in Russia. The country became more vigilant, introducing stricter background checks and ensuring that individuals working with vulnerable populations were closely scrutinized.

Today, Irina Gaidamachuk's name remains synonymous with evil in Russia. Her story serves as a reminder of the darkness that can hide behind seemingly ordinary lives. Those who knew her before her arrest were left questioning how they could have missed the signs, how someone they had seen as a quiet, unassuming woman could have been capable of such horror.

Her case has been studied by criminologists and psychologists alike, as Irina represents a rare but terrifying example of a female serial killer who used manipulation and trust to gain access to her victims. Her cunning and calculated approach to her crimes, paired with her ability to maintain a facade of normalcy, make her one of the most disturbing figures in Russian criminal history.

The legacy of Irina Gaidamachuk is one of fear, mistrust, and caution. She showed the world that evil can wear many faces and that even in the quietest of towns, the deadliest predators may be lurking.

26. A Life of Shadows

On a chilly autumn morning in France, amidst the whispering winds and rustling leaves, the tale of Jeanne Weber began to unfold—a woman whose name would later be tainted by darkness and death. Born on March 6, 1874, in the quiet town of Le Villars, Jeanne's early life did not indicate the notoriety that awaited her. She grew up in a modest home, her father a laborer and her mother a homemaker. Their small cottage, nestled among the rolling hills of rural France, was a place of simple living but also of struggle and hardship.

Jeanne's childhood was marked by poverty. The family barely scraped by, and from an early age, she learned the value of hard work. She helped her mother with the chores and tended to the garden that provided their food. Despite her family's financial struggles, Jeanne found moments of peace in the beauty of the countryside. She would often walk along the meadows, finding comfort in the serene landscape. In these early years, Jeanne developed a passion for art and literature. Though her formal education was limited—she left school at fourteen—her love for books and nature provided her with a rich inner life.

As Jeanne grew into a young woman, she sought to improve her circumstances. At twenty-two, she married Pierre Leroy, a kind-hearted carpenter. They settled into a small cottage near the woods, and soon their first child, a daughter named Marguerite, was born. Jeanne cherished her new role as a mother, but the responsibilities of family life weighed heavily on her. Pierre worked long hours to provide for them, and Jeanne often found herself alone with their child. The isolation and the constant burden of their financial situation began to take a toll on her mental state.

Despite her quiet demeanor, something was unsettling beneath the surface. Jeanne was prone to bouts of melancholy. Her once peaceful walks in the woods became moments of silent turmoil, her thoughts darker, her outlook more despairing. The isolation of rural life only deepened her struggles. The joy she once found in motherhood began to fade, replaced by a creeping sense of dread.

To ease her growing anxiety, Jeanne sought solace in her art. She took up painting, capturing the natural beauty of her surroundings in delicate strokes. Her talent did not go unnoticed. She was praised for her attention to detail, and her ability to evoke emotion in her work. It was a small but significant achievement for Jeanne, giving her a sense of purpose amidst her growing internal conflict. Her reputation as a talented artist spread, and she began receiving commissions from local families and patrons.

Yet even as her artistic career blossomed, darkness continued to seep into her life. Pierre, once the sturdy rock of their household, fell ill. His health declined rapidly, leaving Jeanne to care for him while managing the household. The pressure mounted. With no means of steady income beyond her sporadic commissions, the family's financial situation worsened. It seemed that no matter how hard she tried, the weight of life's burdens pressed down on her with unrelenting force.

Amidst these challenges, Jeanne began volunteering at a local orphanage. She taught painting classes to underprivileged children, hoping to share her love for art with them. She was seen as a kind and gentle woman, deeply compassionate toward the young and the needy. But it was during her time at the orphanage that a series of inexplicable tragedies began to occur.

Over several months, infants under Jeanne's care began to die mysteriously. At first, the deaths were attributed to illness—sudden, tragic but not unheard of in a time when infant mortality was high. But as more and more children perished, whispers of suspicion began to spread. How could it be that so many infants, healthy just days before, suddenly fell gravely ill? The authorities were alerted, and an investigation was launched.

The news of Jeanne's involvement in the infant deaths shocked the community. How could this woman, so soft-spoken and nurturing, be responsible for such horrors? Neighbors, who had once admired her, were now filled with doubt. Some still defended her, refusing to believe that someone who had shown such kindness could be capable of such cruelty. Others began to wonder if the dark melancholy they had noticed in Jeanne was not just sadness, but something far more sinister.

The trial that followed was sensational. The media portrayed Jeanne as a villain, dubbing her "The Ogress of the Goutte d'Or," a name that reflected the growing belief that she had murdered the infants under her care. Jeanne, for her part, maintained her innocence. She sat quietly through the proceedings, her face pale and expressionless. When asked why so many infants had died, she simply shrugged and said, "It was not my doing."

Despite her claims of innocence, the evidence against her was damning. Several witnesses testified to her strange behavior, noting how she had often been the last person to see the infants alive. Doctors presented evidence suggesting that the children had not died of natural causes, but rather had been smothered. It became clear that the deaths were no coincidence.

In the end, Jeanne Weber was convicted of multiple murders. She was sentenced to life in prison, where she would spend the remainder of her days. Even behind bars, she maintained her innocence, though she never explained the deaths. To this day, some believe Jeanne may have suffered from a psychological disorder, one that drove her to commit the unthinkable acts while in a dissociated state. Others argue that she was fully aware of her actions and that her crimes were motivated by a deep-seated desire for control over life and death.

As she languished in prison, the once-bright spark of Jeanne's artistic talent was extinguished. She no longer painted, no longer walked through the woods, or sketched the landscapes she had once loved. Her life, once filled with small joys, had been consumed by darkness.

Years after her death, Jeanne's story remains a source of fascination and horror. Historians and criminologists alike have debated her motivations, with some viewing her as a cold-blooded murderer, and others as a tragic figure driven to madness by a lifetime of hardship and neglect. Her legacy is a reminder of the fragility of the human mind, of the thin line that separates ordinary life from unspeakable acts of violence.

Today, Jeanne Weber's name is remembered not for her artistic achievements, but for the lives she took. Her story, like the quiet autumn mornings of her youth, is tinged with sadness and shadow—a life that could have been so different, had it not been for the darkness that took hold of her soul.

27. Descent into Darkness

In the misty moors of England, where fog curls around ancient oaks and whispers secrets through the reeds, the story of Joanna Dennehy began—a chilling tale that would send shockwaves across the country. Born on September 5, 1982, in St Albans, a picturesque town in Hertfordshire, Joanna was not marked by anything extraordinary at birth. But her journey into infamy was one that no one could have predicted.

Joanna grew up in a household filled with turbulence. Her parents' marriage was fraught with conflict, and the instability of their relationship left a deep impression on her young mind. The financial struggles, constant relocations, and emotional strain fostered a sense of disconnection from her family. This fractured childhood would sow the seeds of rebellion and anger that would later fuel her destructive path.

Her academic life mirrored the chaos at home. Joanna moved between schools, never settling long enough to form lasting friendships or a sense of belonging. She found herself drawn to the company of outcasts, people who, like her, pushed back against societal norms. Academically, she floundered. The rigid structures of education clashed with her desire for freedom, leading her to drop out early and seek solace in more dangerous pursuits.

As a teenager, Joanna spiraled into a world of substance abuse and reckless behavior. Her once-innocent curiosity about the macabre grew into an obsession with the darker side of life. She consumed crime novels, fascinated by the minds of those who committed violent acts. Beneath her outward defiance, there was a deep well of inner turmoil—a battle with demons that would soon manifest in horrifying ways.

Her relationship with her parents, particularly her mother, became strained. There were frequent clashes over her lifestyle, with Joanna refusing to conform to any of the expectations placed upon her. By the time she reached her early twenties, Joanna had already started to exhibit signs of a deeper psychological conflict. She sought out toxic relationships, often gravitating towards individuals who shared her self-destructive tendencies.

It was during this period that she met men who would later become accomplices in her grisly crimes. Her manipulative nature allowed her to exert control over those around her, and her charm masked the growing storm of violence that lurked beneath. Joanna's relationships were volatile, filled with intense highs and devastating lows. The birth of her two children did little to ground her; instead, her chaotic lifestyle continued unabated.

Joanna's fascination with violence soon escalated. She began expressing darker thoughts, sharing fantasies of harming others with those she trusted. For those around her, these were disturbing red flags, but no one could foresee the horrific path she was about to take.

In 2013, Joanna's descent into full-blown murder began. Her first victim was Lukasz Slaboszewski, a man she had lured with promises of companionship. Joanna had a way of making people feel at ease, masking her true intentions with ease. When the moment came, she stabbed him repeatedly, later bragging about how the thrill of killing gave her a sense of power. The brutality of the attack shocked even those close to her, but Joanna felt nothing but exhilaration.

Soon after, she killed two more men, John Chapman, and Kevin Lee, in similarly violent ways. The killings were senseless, random acts of brutality that left investigators baffled. The bodies of her victims were discarded carelessly, as though they were mere objects to her. Joanna showed no remorse—she even took pleasure in the fear and chaos her actions caused.

As the murders continued, Joanna embarked on a spree that left the nation in shock. Her actions were not motivated by financial gain, revenge, or personal animosity—she killed simply because she wanted to. Her lack of empathy, her cold detachment, and her desire to control others led experts to diagnose her with psychopathic tendencies. Joanna reveled in the attention, smiling and laughing even as her victims' bodies were being discovered.

The trial that followed Joanna's arrest was one of the most high-profile cases in recent British history. The public struggled to comprehend how a woman, a mother, could be capable of such horrifying acts. During the trial, Joanna remained indifferent, even smirking as the gruesome details of her crimes were read aloud. When asked why she committed the murders, Joanna coldly replied, "I killed to see how it felt."

Her lack of remorse shocked the courtroom. Psychologists who analyzed Joanna described her as one of the most dangerous individuals they had ever encountered. Her willingness to kill without hesitation, coupled with her ability to manipulate those around her, made her a truly terrifying figure.

Joanna was sentenced to life in prison without the possibility of parole, ensuring that she would never again have the opportunity to harm another person. But even as the doors of the prison closed behind her, the legacy of her crimes continued to haunt those who had followed the case.

For the families of her victims, there was no closure. The senseless nature of Joanna's actions made the loss of their loved ones even harder to bear. Communities across England were left reeling from the idea that someone so seemingly ordinary could harbor such profound darkness.

In the years since her conviction, Joanna's case has been studied extensively by criminologists and psychologists, all seeking to understand what drove her to commit such heinous acts. Was it her troubled upbringing, her mental instability, or simply an inherent capacity for evil? The answer remains elusive, but what is certain is that Joanna Dennehy's story serves as a grim reminder of the darkness that can lurk beneath the surface of the human psyche.

Her actions forced society to confront uncomfortable questions about mental illness, societal responsibility, and the nature of evil itself. Could her crimes have been prevented with early intervention? Did the system fail to provide the support she needed to stop her descent into madness? These are questions that continue to linger long after Joanna is locked away.

The scars left by Joanna Dennehy's crimes will never fully heal. Her victims' families still grapple with their loss, and the communities she terrorized remain haunted by the memory of her brutality. Her name, once unknown, is now synonymous with horror—a chilling reminder of the capacity for violence that exists within even the most seemingly ordinary individuals.

Joanna Dennehy's legacy is not one of greatness or redemption but of infamy. Her story compels society to examine its failings, to ask how someone like her could slip through the cracks unnoticed. In the end, she remains a figure of revulsion and morbid fascination—a reminder of the fragile line between sanity and madness, and the devastating consequences when that line is crossed.

28. The Dark Nurse

In the bustling streets of 19th-century Boston, amidst the clangor of industry and the whispers of societal change, lived a woman who would soon be known as Jolly Jane Toppan. Her friendly demeanor, warm smile, and kind presence masked a dark and twisted soul that would leave a trail of death and betrayal. Her story is one of the most chilling in American history, making her infamous as a nurse who took lives rather than saving them.

Born Honora Kelley on March 31, 1854, in Boston, Massachusetts, Jane's early years were shaped by tragedy. Her mother, Brigid Kelley, died when she was very young, and her father, Peter Kelley, struggled with mental illness. Jane and her siblings grew up in poverty, surviving in the harsh urban streets of Boston. Her father's erratic behavior led to him abandoning his children at an orphanage. Jane was left to fend for herself in a world that showed her little kindness. The instability and neglect she experienced during her childhood planted the seeds for the darkness that would soon define her life.

As a child, Jane was sent to live with the Toppan family, who took her in as an indentured servant. She took their last name, and it was in this home that the persona of "Jolly Jane" began to form. Despite her challenging upbringing, she was known for her cheerful demeanor. She excelled in her duties, and by all appearances, seemed to be a loyal and content servant. However, beneath the surface, there was a growing desire for control, attention, and perhaps revenge against the world that had been so unkind to her.

As she grew older, Jane found work as a nurse, a profession that would give her access to the most vulnerable: the sick and the dying. She attended nursing school at Cambridge Hospital, where she quickly became a favorite among patients and staff. Her easy smile and comforting presence earned her the nickname "Jolly Jane." No one could have imagined that beneath that friendly exterior was a woman who would soon use her skills for something far more sinister.

Jane had a fascination with the power she held over life and death. Her interest in medicine wasn't driven solely by a desire to help others; it was driven by a dark curiosity. She began experimenting on her patients, using them as test subjects for her own morbid pleasure. She administered lethal doses of morphine and atropine, watching carefully as her victims slipped into unconsciousness. Sometimes, she would bring them back from the brink of death, just to repeat the process. The line between life and death was something Jane controlled, and she reveled in that power.

Her victims were often elderly, vulnerable patients who trusted her completely. She killed with a chilling indifference, using her knowledge of drugs to ensure her crimes went undetected. Jane's methods were meticulous—administering just enough poison to mimic natural causes. Her medical colleagues and supervisors never suspected her of wrongdoing. In fact, she was often praised for her dedication and excellent bedside manner.

For years, Jane continued her killing spree without raising suspicion. She moved from hospital to hospital, leaving behind a trail of mysterious deaths. Her ability to blend into society, to be charming and beloved while committing heinous crimes, made her one of the most dangerous types of killers. She took the trust placed in her by her patients and used it against them.

As Jane's crimes escalated, so did her confidence. She no longer limited herself to hospital patients. She began killing people outside her professional life, targeting friends and acquaintances. She killed the wife of her landlord and even members of her foster family. Her personal vendettas became intertwined with her desire for control. Killing was no longer just about curiosity—it was about dominance. She admitted later that her motivation was simple: "I had a desire to kill more people—helpless people."

The turning point came when Jane murdered one of her close friends, Elizabeth Brigham, with whom she had developed an intense jealousy. Elizabeth had everything Jane wanted—a stable life, a loving family—and that envy drove Jane to poison her. After Elizabeth's death, Jane ingratiated herself with the grieving family, even attempting to seduce Elizabeth's widower. Her twisted need for attention knew no bounds.

But as Jane's crimes became more reckless, people began to notice the pattern of deaths that seemed to follow her wherever she went. Suspicion finally caught up with her when the Davis family, relatives of one of her victims, demanded an autopsy. The results confirmed their worst fears: their loved one had been poisoned.

Jane was arrested in 1901, and during her trial, the public learned the full extent of her horrific crimes. Jane confessed to killing at least 31 people, though many believe the number was much higher. She admitted to deriving pleasure from the act of killing, something she described with eerie nonchalance. Her confessions were chilling in their simplicity, as though taking a life was no different than taking a breath.

During her trial, Jane's defense team attempted to argue that she was insane, pointing to her troubled childhood and history of mental instability. In court, she was described as a woman who killed "for the joy and excitement of it." Psychologists at the time concluded that Jane was a textbook example of a sociopath—a person completely devoid of empathy, driven solely by self-gratification and power.

Jane's chilling lack of remorse shocked the nation. She was found not guilty because of insanity and was committed to Taunton Insane Hospital, where she would spend the rest of her life. Even in confinement, Jane remained eerily cheerful, earning her the title "Jolly Jane" among the staff. She lived out her days in the institution, never fully comprehending the terror she had inflicted on so many lives.

Jane Toppan's legacy is one of horror and betrayal. She was a nurse, someone trusted to care for the sick and vulnerable, but she used that trust as a weapon. Her story is a stark reminder of the thin line between caregiver and predator, and the devastating consequences when that line is crossed.

Her case prompted widespread reforms in healthcare, particularly in the oversight and monitoring of medical professionals. Jane's crimes exposed the vulnerabilities within the system, prompting changes in background checks and the way medical staff were supervised. The fear that someone like her could slip through the cracks and commit such heinous acts led to new standards in patient care and safety protocols that are still in place today.

The story of Jolly Jane Toppan continues to haunt the annals of crime history. Her smiling face and caring demeanor masked a profound evil that took pleasure in the suffering of others. In the end, her legacy serves as a chilling reminder of the darkness that can lurk behind even the most trusted faces and the importance of vigilance in safeguarding those who cannot protect themselves.

29. The Dark Killer

I n the heart of Mexico City, where the streets pulse with life, music, and the scent of street food, a chilling story unfolded. A woman, Juana Barraza, whose gentle demeanor concealed a horrific secret, would go on to become one of Mexico's most feared criminals. Known as "La Mataviejitas," or "The Old Lady Killer," her name would forever be linked to a series of brutal murders that shocked the nation and left a lasting scar on Mexican society.

Born on December 27, 1957, in the small, arid town of Hidalgo, Juana's early life was shaped by poverty, instability, and hardship. Her family's adobe home stood against the vast and sun-scorched landscape, with every day a battle for survival. Her parents struggled, often moving to find work, and Juana grew up quickly, shouldering responsibilities beyond her years.

Juana's childhood was difficult, filled with moments of neglect and sadness. Her mother, a harsh and cold woman, was an alcoholic who reportedly traded her young daughter to a man for a few bottles of beer. The trauma of that betrayal haunted Juana and shaped her perception of the world around her. While her formal education was brief—interrupted by the need to help with chores and take care of her younger siblings—Juana possessed a sharp mind and a quiet determination. But beneath her resilience lay a deep and growing sense of anger.

As a young woman, Juana sought escape through marriage, but her relationships were marked by volatility. She married young, and had several children, but found no stability in these unions. Her marriages were turbulent, filled with financial struggles and constant tension. Despite this, Juana took on various jobs, from a street vendor to a domestic worker, and even a professional wrestler, adopting the stage name "La Dama del Silencio" (The Lady of Silence). Wrestling became an outlet for her frustrations, but it wasn't enough to ease the deep wounds of her past.

Beneath her outward appearance of strength and independence, Juana's resentment festered. She felt the weight of her hardships bearing down on her, and her resentment toward her mother, combined with the memories of her abuse, simmered dangerously beneath the surface. The elderly woman she would later target reminded her of her mother—vulnerable, frail, and, in her mind, deserving of the anger she couldn't release.

Her descent into murder began slowly, methodically. Working as a caregiver for elderly women, Juana found herself in a position of trust. She would befriend her victims, gaining access to their homes under the guise of helping them, only to later strike when they were most vulnerable. Her preferred method was strangulation, often using objects found within their homes—scarves, cords, or whatever was at hand. She would rob her victims after killing them and taking small valuables, though her crimes were more about power and control than money.

Between the late 1990s and early 2000s, Juana Barraza's crimes escalated. Elderly women were being found strangled in their homes, and their lifeless bodies were discovered by neighbors or family members. The police were slow to connect the dots, at first attributing the murders to several different criminals. The randomness of the killings and the careful way Juana executed her crimes made her difficult to catch. She was like a ghost, slipping through the streets of Mexico City without leaving a trace.

Fear spread through the city's elderly population. Rumors of a serial killer targeting older women caused widespread panic. Women who had spent their entire lives walking freely now locked their doors in fear. The newspapers began dubbing the mysterious killer "La Mataviejitas." For years, Juana evaded capture, blending into society with ease, her actions hidden behind the facade of a compassionate caregiver.

Juana's double life was masterfully crafted. On the one hand, she appeared to be a hardworking, unassuming woman, living a life of modesty and dedication to her family. But on the other hand, she was a cold-blooded killer, driven by anger and a need for revenge. The psychological toll of her childhood trauma, combined with her bitter resentment toward her mother, drove her to take out her pain on innocent elderly women who, in her mind, symbolized her abusers.

In 2006, Juana's killing spree finally came to an end. She was caught after the murder of an elderly woman named Ana María de los Reyes, who had been strangled with a stethoscope. Juana was seen leaving the scene of the crime by a witness, and the description led to her arrest. When the authorities searched her home, they found objects stolen from her victims, confirming the horrific truth. Juana Barraza, the woman who had eluded them for so long, was indeed La Mataviejitas.

During her trial, Juana's history came to light, and the media seized upon the story of her troubled childhood and difficult life. But despite the explanations offered for her behavior, the sheer brutality of her crimes could not be ignored. She confessed to at least 16 murders, though authorities believe she may have been responsible for as many as 40. Her cold and emotionless demeanor during the trial shocked the nation. She showed no remorse for her actions, calmly recounting her crimes with a chilling detachment.

The public was left grappling with the question: How could a woman—someone trusted to care for the elderly—commit such horrific acts? The story of Juana Barraza struck a nerve in Mexico, revealing the deep flaws in the social systems that allowed vulnerable populations, particularly elderly women, to slip through the cracks. Her case sparked outrage and led to reforms aimed at improving the safety and security of seniors, as well as a reevaluation of how caregivers were hired and monitored.

Forensic psychologists who studied Juana's case pointed to her traumatic upbringing as a major factor in her descent into murder. Her unresolved childhood trauma, combined with the pressures of poverty and the failure of her relationships, created a perfect storm of rage and resentment. Juana's victims, though innocent, became symbolic targets for the pain she could never direct at her real tormentors.

Juana Barraza's legacy is one of fear, sorrow, and unresolved questions. She remains a polarizing figure in Mexican history, remembered both for her chilling crimes and the broader societal issues her case highlighted. Her story continues to fascinate criminologists and psychologists alike, who seek to understand the mind of a killer shaped by hardship and tragedy.

Today, Juana Barraza sits in prison, serving a life sentence for her crimes. Her name is etched in Mexico's history as one of its most infamous serial killers, a woman whose outward calm hid a deep well of anger and a desire for revenge. Her story is a haunting reminder of the darkness that can grow in the heart of someone who feels abandoned by the world. As the city of Mexico slowly healed from the fear she instilled, her tale continues to serve as a cautionary reflection on the complexities of human nature and the far-reaching consequences of trauma left unchecked.

30. The Betrayal of Trust

In the peaceful town of Northampton, Massachusetts, where the seasons transform the landscape with rich hues and crisp air, Kristen Gilbert walked among her peers as a trusted nurse. Her white uniform symbolized care, her smile radiated warmth, and her dedication to her patients seemed unwavering. Yet beneath this surface of compassion and professionalism, Kristen harbored a dark secret that would eventually unfold into one of the most shocking medical serial killer cases in American history.

Kristen Heather Strickland was born on November 13, 1967, in Fall River, Massachusetts. The turbulent autumn weather seemed to mirror the complexity of her future life. Born into what appeared to be a loving family, her early years offered no hint of the path she would later choose. Her parents, William and Claudia Strickland, raised Kristen alongside her two siblings in the comfortable suburbs of Massachusetts. By all accounts, Kristen had a stable upbringing, marked by curiosity, academic success, and a budding interest in science.

From a young age, Kristen excelled in school. Her teachers praised her sharp intellect, particularly in math and science, which naturally led her toward a healthcare career. Her desire to make a difference and her fascination with the medical field led her to pursue a career as a nurse. At first glance, her life seemed to be following the path of success and service. She worked hard, earned her qualifications, and eventually married Glenn Gilbert, a fellow healthcare professional. Together, they built a home and started a family.

However, beneath the picture-perfect life, cracks began to show. Kristen's marriage was fraught with tension, and her career as a nurse—once a calling—became a source of frustration and pressure. The demands of balancing her career with her responsibilities as a wife and mother weighed heavily on her, and Kristen began to unravel. What should have been a life of care and compassion twisted into something far more sinister.

Kristen's descent into darkness began quietly, unnoticed by those around her. She found herself drawn to the power that came with her position as a nurse. She could save lives, but that power also came with the terrifying ability to end them. It started with small manipulations of patient care, and subtle adjustments that caused patients to spiral into medical emergencies. Kristen would then swoop in, appearing to save the day, relishing the attention and praise from her colleagues. It was a dangerous game, one fueled by her craving for control and recognition.

At the Veterans Affairs Medical Center in Northampton, where she worked, Kristen became known as a dedicated nurse who could handle the most critical cases. She was calm under pressure, attentive to her patients, and always ready to help in a crisis. What no one realized was that many of these crises were of her own making. Using epinephrine, a drug that increases heart rate and can induce cardiac arrest in high doses, Kristen began administering lethal amounts to her patients. She created emergencies so she could rush in, play the hero, and bask in the admiration of her colleagues.

The deaths started to pile up. Elderly veterans who had come to the VA hospital for care suddenly deteriorated and died in ways that were difficult to explain. The atmosphere in the hospital grew tense as staff struggled to understand the rising number of cardiac arrests, but Kristen remained calm and composed, continuing her deadly work. For years, no one suspected the quiet nurse with the sweet smile.

Her manipulation of the medical system was as meticulous as it was terrifying. She knew how to alter medical records to cover her tracks, how to appear genuinely concerned, and how to manipulate her colleagues and supervisors into trusting her completely. Kristen's ability to blend into the environment, to exploit the very system designed to care for the most vulnerable, made her an invisible predator.

However, as the death toll mounted, whispers of suspicion began to circulate. Nurses and doctors started to notice a pattern—whenever Kristen was on duty, patients seemed more likely to suffer unexplained emergencies. The once-admired nurse was now the subject of quiet conversations in break rooms, but no one had any proof.

It wasn't until 1996, when the suspicious deaths caught the attention of hospital administrators and law enforcement, that the investigation into Kristen Gilbert truly began. The atmosphere in the hospital grew heavy with anxiety as investigators combed through records and interviewed staff. Kristen, sensing that the net was closing in, tried to maintain her innocence, but cracks began to appear in her facade. Rumors of her involvement in the deaths spread, and soon, the unthinkable truth began to emerge.

Kristen was arrested, and her trial became a national spectacle. As details of the case unfolded, the public was horrified by the revelations. Kristen had manipulated the trust of her patients and colleagues, using her position to kill the very people she had sworn to care for. Her crimes raised disturbing questions about the vulnerabilities within the healthcare system and the ease with which someone could exploit that trust for personal gain.

During the trial, Kristen maintained a calm and calculated demeanor, even as she was confronted with the evidence of her actions. Her motives were chillingly simple—she craved attention and control. Her actions were not driven by financial gain or revenge but by the thrill of manipulating life and death. It was this chilling detachment from the suffering she caused that left many speechless.

In 2001, Kristen Gilbert was convicted of four counts of murder and two counts of attempted murder. She was sentenced to life in prison without the possibility of parole. The trial was a grim reminder of the dangers posed by those who abuse positions of trust and authority for their own twisted purposes.

The aftermath of Kristen's crimes sent shockwaves through the healthcare community. Hospitals across the country reassessed their protocols, implementing stricter monitoring and oversight to prevent similar tragedies from happening again. The case also prompted discussions about the psychological screening of healthcare professionals, with a greater emphasis on identifying those who might pose a danger to their patients.

For those who knew Kristen, the revelation of her true nature was devastating. Colleagues who had worked side by side with her struggled to reconcile the compassionate nurse they thought they knew with the cold-blooded killer she had become. Her family, too, was left grappling with the horror of her actions, their once-beloved daughter now a symbol of betrayal and death.

Kristen Gilbert's story is a haunting reminder of the fragility of trust. Her ability to mask her true intentions behind a facade of professionalism allowed her to commit her crimes for years without detection. She exploited the very system meant to protect patients, turning it into her personal playground of manipulation and death. In the end, her legacy is not one of healing or compassion, but of betrayal and destruction.

Kristen's crimes continue to provoke debate and reflection within the medical community and beyond. How could someone so trusted commit such horrific acts? What signs were missed? How can we prevent this from happening again? These are the questions that linger, even as the years pass since Kristen's conviction.

Today, Kristen Gilbert sits in a prison cell, her once-bright future now reduced to a dark chapter in American history. Her story remains a sobering reminder of the dangers posed by those who abuse positions of trust for personal gain. Her name is etched in the annals of crime and justice as a chilling example of the evil that can hide behind even the most innocent of faces.

31. The Dark Charm

In the heart of early 19th-century Charleston, South Carolina, Lavinia Fisher walked with a charm that few could resist. The streets bustled with traders, sailors, and travelers, and the oaks hung with moss swayed in the thick, humid air. Lavinia, alongside her husband John, owned the Six Mile Wayfarer House, an inn that welcomed guests traveling the roads just outside Charleston. But behind the warm smiles and welcoming facade, something far more sinister lurked. Lavinia would soon be remembered not for her beauty or hospitality, but for the blood that stained her hands and the lives that were lost under her roof.

Lavinia was born in 1793, in the lush, green Lowcountry of South Carolina. Her early life is shrouded in mystery. Little is known about her childhood or the family that raised her, but by the time she reached adulthood, Lavinia had developed a charisma that could charm anyone who crossed her path. She was known for her sharp wit and beauty, traits that would later aid her in committing unthinkable crimes.

It was in Charleston where she met John Fisher, a man whose charm matched her own, and together they became a couple bound by love, greed, and a shared hunger for more than life seemed to offer. They opened the Six Mile Wayfarer House, an inn that became a popular stop for travelers passing through Charleston. But the guests who checked in often didn't check out.

The Fishers lived in a time when travelers were easy targets. Roads were dangerous, and many people traveled alone with no one knowing their whereabouts. Lavinia, with her bewitching smile and soothing words, played the perfect hostess. John was a solid, dependable partner. Together, they provided a sense of safety and comfort, a refuge for weary guests.

But that refuge soon became a trap. Lavinia would offer weary travelers a hot meal, sweet tea, and a place to rest their heads. She'd charm them with conversation, make them feel at ease. Once they were lulled into a false sense of security, the trap was set. The Fishers devised a cruel method of murder: poisoning their guests' food or drink and, at times, using a specially rigged bed with a trapdoor that would send victims plunging into the cellar below.

The couple's crimes went unnoticed for years. Travelers would disappear, but the roads were perilous, and people often went missing. It wasn't until 1819 that rumors of the Fishers' murderous activities began to circulate. People started to whisper that travelers who stayed at their inn were never seen again. Authorities were slow to act, not believing that such a kind and welcoming couple could be responsible for the disappearances.

But Lavinia and John Fisher's luck eventually ran out. A man named David Ross, staying at their inn one evening, narrowly escaped death. Suspicious of Lavinia's strange behavior and the unsettling atmosphere at the inn, Ross fled in the night. He alerted the authorities, and soon the Fishers' dark secret was revealed.

When law enforcement raided the Six Mile Wayfarer House, they discovered more than just empty rooms. Beneath the inn lay a macabre sight—evidence of the couple's crimes, including belongings of the missing travelers. Though the exact number of their victims remains unknown, the horror was undeniable.

Lavinia and John were arrested, and their trial became the talk of Charleston. The people who once marveled at Lavinia's beauty and charm now saw her for what she truly was—a woman capable of cold-blooded murder. Despite her pleas of innocence, the evidence against the Fishers was overwhelming. The tales of her manipulation, her use of charm to lure victims, and the calculated nature of her crimes shocked the city.

During the trial, Lavinia remained defiant. Her beauty still captivated, even as she faced the gallows. She refused to show remorse for her actions, and rumors circulated that she believed she would escape execution because she was a woman. But justice, it seemed, would not be swayed by her charms.

On the day of their execution in 1820, John Fisher went to his death quietly, asking for forgiveness. Lavinia, however, did not go gently. Dressed in her wedding gown, she hoped to marry death as her final partner. Before the noose tightened around her neck, she reportedly shouted to the crowd, "If you have a message you want to send to hell, give it to me—I'll carry it." With those chilling words, Lavinia Fisher's life came to a violent end.

Lavinia's death did not mark the end of her story. Her legend only grew in the years following her execution. Tales of her ghost haunting Charleston's Old City Jail, where she was held before her execution, have become part of

Southern folklore. Some claim to have seen her spirit, still dressed in white, wandering the jail's dark halls, her beauty now a ghostly remnant of the woman who lured so many to their deaths.

But beyond the ghost stories and the folklore, Lavinia Fisher's legacy serves as a dark reminder of the dangers of unchecked trust and the consequences of letting greed and cruelty guide one's actions. The Fishers had turned their inn, a place meant to offer safety and rest, into a house of horrors. Their crimes shook Charleston to its core and left a lasting impact on the city's history.

Today, Lavinia Fisher remains a figure of both fear and fascination. Her name is etched into the dark history of American crime, a reminder that evil can wear a friendly smile and offer you a cup of tea. The mystery surrounding her true motives, the extent of her crimes, and her cold-blooded nature have cemented her place as one of America's first—and most infamous—female serial killers.

As the years pass, her tale continues to captivate those who are drawn to the shadows of history, where reality and legend blur, and where Lavinia Fisher, with her chilling beauty and deadly charm, reigns as a Southern Gothic icon.

32. The Dark Legacy

In the peaceful countryside of southern Italy, where olive groves stretch towards the horizon and the warm winds sweep over the hills, lived Leonarda Cianciulli, a woman whose story would become one of the most horrifying in the country's history. Born amidst the simplicity of rural life in 1894, Leonarda's childhood was not one of fairy tales or innocence but of hardship, superstition, and isolation. From this humble beginning would emerge a woman consumed by a terrifying belief—that murder was the only way to protect those she loved.

Leonarda was born in Montella, a small village in the Avellino province of Italy. Her early years were shaped by poverty and an unstable home. The rugged hills and quiet fields that surrounded her life were a stark contrast to the turmoil inside her. Her mother, embittered by her own hardships, often treated Leonarda with cruelty. As a child, Leonarda was a witness to the rural superstitions that permeated the villages—omens, curses, and folk rituals were part of everyday life. She grew up believing in the dark forces that could control fate and shape destinies.

From an early age, Leonarda was convinced she had been cursed. Her mother had allegedly cursed her during one of their many arguments, and from that moment, Leonarda believed she would face nothing but tragedy in her life. And tragedy did follow her. Her first marriage, one arranged by her family, quickly fell apart, and after defying her parents to marry the man she loved—Raffaele Pansardi—Leonarda found herself on a path of even greater misery. The couple moved to Correggio, a town in Northern Italy, and though they seemed to have built a stable life together, dark clouds loomed over them.

It was in Correggio where the true horror of Leonarda's life began to unfold. After experiencing several miscarriages and losing three children in infancy, Leonarda became obsessed with the idea of protecting her remaining children. Desperate to shield them from harm, her already fragile mental state deteriorated. The weight of her tragedies and superstitions began to twist her thinking, leading her down a path that few could have anticipated.

The looming shadow of World War II intensified her fears. Her son, Giuseppe, whom she adored, was conscripted to fight in the Italian army.

Paralyzed by the thought of losing him, Leonarda turned to the only solution she believed would save him—human sacrifice. Leonarda had long been fascinated by the occult and dark rituals. She believed that the only way to prevent her son's death was to offer lives in exchange for his safety. She became convinced that the blood of others would protect her child.

In 1939, Leonarda lured her first victim to her home. Faustina Setti, a lonely woman in her fifties, sought Leonarda's advice in finding a husband. Leonarda, known in the town for her skills in palmistry and fortune-telling, promised to help her. She convinced Faustina to travel to another town to meet her prospective suitor, but first, Leonarda invited her to her home. Faustina drank a glass of wine that Leonarda had laced with poison. When the poison took effect, Leonarda struck, killing Faustina in her kitchen. She dismembered the body, boiling it down to make soap. With a disturbing efficiency, Leonarda melted her victim's remains into bars of soap and even turned some of the remains into teacakes, which she shared with neighbors.

Despite the horror of the crime, Leonarda felt no remorse. In her mind, the sacrifice was necessary. She believed she was performing a ritual that would protect her son, and her belief was strong enough to silence any moral doubt.

But one victim was not enough. Leonarda's desperation for protection only grew. In 1940, she found her next victim, Francesca Soavi. Like Faustina, Francesca was seeking Leonarda's help. She was promised a job at a girls' school in another town, but instead of opportunity, Francesca met the same fate as Leonarda's first victim. Poisoned, killed, and dismembered, Francesca's remains were also turned into soap and teacakes.

Leonarda's third and final victim, Virginia Cacioppo, was a former opera singer. Virginia's life had taken a turn for the worse, and she too sought Leonarda's guidance. As with the others, Leonarda lured her in with promises of a better life, but instead, Virginia's life ended violently in Leonarda's kitchen. This time, however, Leonarda used Virginia's remains to make soap that she claimed was the finest she had ever made.

For a time, Leonarda's crimes went unnoticed. The women she killed were not missed by many, and Leonarda's reputation in the community shielded her from suspicion. She was known as a devoted mother and a helpful neighbor. No one could have imagined the horrific truth behind her façade.

But Leonarda's downfall came when Virginia's sister grew suspicious of her sudden disappearance. She reported her concerns to the police, who began an investigation. It didn't take long for the authorities to connect the dots, and in 1940, Leonarda was arrested. During her trial, Leonarda showed no signs of guilt. She freely confessed to the murders, detailing the gruesome acts with a chilling lack of emotion. She remained steadfast in her belief that the sacrifices were necessary to protect her children.

The courtroom was stunned by her confessions. People were horrified by her calm demeanor and the graphic details of her crimes. Leonarda was sentenced to 30 years in prison and three years in a criminal asylum, where she eventually died in 1970.

Leonarda Cianciulli's crimes shocked Italy and the world. Her story was a chilling reminder of how deep superstition and fear could drive someone to commit unimaginable acts. Behind the mask of a loving mother and trusted neighbor lurked a mind consumed by terror and dark beliefs. She truly believed that by sacrificing others, she could save her child's life, and in that belief, she found a way to justify the most heinous of deeds.

Today, Leonarda Cianciulli's name is synonymous with horror. Her actions, driven by superstition and maternal obsession, serve as a dark chapter in the annals of crime. The "Soap-Maker of Correggio" is remembered not only for the brutality of her crimes but for the disturbing reasons behind them. She remains a figure both feared and pitied, a woman whose desperation to protect her family led her to unimaginable cruelty.

33. The Dark Arts

In the shadowy streets of ancient Rome, where marble pillars glistened in the hot Mediterranean sun and the whispers of political ambition echoed through the halls of power, there lived a woman whose name would forever be etched into the city's infamous history—Locusta, the poisoner. Her story, one woven into the very fabric of Roman intrigue, tells of a woman who used her knowledge of deadly herbs and toxins to shape the fate of emperors and nobles alike.

Locusta's origins are shrouded in mystery. Born sometime during the reign of Emperor Claudius in the 1st century AD, little is known of her family or her early life. What is clear, however, is that Locusta possessed a unique and dangerous skill—an almost supernatural ability to concoct poisons from plants, roots, and animal venoms. Her keen intellect and knowledge of herbalism set her apart from the common people of Rome, marking her as a woman destined for a darker path.

The bustling streets of Rome filled with traders, merchants, and noblemen, became the backdrop for Locusta's ascent. Growing up in the chaotic heart of the empire, she may have experienced poverty and uncertainty, but she quickly learned how to navigate the complex social web of the city. Her education was not traditional; rather than learning the arts of rhetoric or philosophy, Locusta was trained in the subtle and secretive art of poison-making. She studied under the guidance of herbalists and those who operated in the underworld, perfecting her craft in the shadows.

It wasn't long before her talents caught the attention of powerful figures in Roman society. While many viewed her as a mere witch or an herbalist, others saw her for what she truly was—an assassin capable of eliminating rivals without leaving a trace. Locusta's early career was built in these shadows, working for wealthy patrons who needed a discreet solution to their problems. Her poisons were efficient and deadly, capable of mimicking natural illnesses and leaving few clues behind.

But her rise to infamy truly began with her involvement in the highest echelons of Roman power. Agrippina the Younger, mother of the future Emperor Nero, sought Locusta's services in a deadly plot. Agrippina had a grand ambition: to place her son on the throne, but Emperor Claudius, her husband, stood in the way. To ensure Nero's ascension, Claudius needed to die.

It was in this treacherous plot that Locusta made her name. In 54 AD, she prepared a deadly poison for Claudius, carefully crafting a concoction that would kill the emperor slowly, mimicking the symptoms of food poisoning. When Claudius consumed the poisoned dish, his death appeared almost natural, and Agrippina's plot succeeded. With Claudius dead, Nero ascended to the throne, and Locusta became an indispensable tool in the deadly game of Roman politics.

Nero, a young and unstable ruler, quickly found a use for Locusta's talents. His rule was threatened by Britannicus, the legitimate son of Claudius and rightful heir to the throne. Locusta was once again called upon to remove this obstacle. In 55 AD, she prepared another fatal poison, this time lacing Britannicus's drink. During a feast, the young boy took a sip, and moments later, he collapsed, writhing in pain. The poison had worked flawlessly, and Nero's position as emperor was secured.

Locusta's ability to carry out these high-profile assassinations with such skill and discretion made her both feared and revered. As her reputation grew, she became Nero's personal poisoner, at his beck and call whenever a rival needed to be eliminated. In exchange for her services, Locusta was granted wealth, land, and protection, but she lived with the constant threat of betrayal. In Rome, alliances were as fragile as glass, and the hand that gave her gold one day could turn against her the next.

But Locusta was not merely a tool of the powerful; she was a woman of cunning and intelligence, aware of the dangerous game she was playing. The corridors of power in Rome were filled with whispers of treachery, and Locusta knew that one wrong move could lead to her downfall. Her skill in poison-making was matched by her ability to remain in the shadows, never drawing too much attention to herself.

Despite her success, Locusta's position became increasingly precarious. Nero's reign was marked by chaos and paranoia, and his growing instability made him a dangerous master. He trusted no one, not even his closest allies, and Locusta's continued service to him only deepened her involvement in the empire's blood-soaked politics.

In the years following Britannicus's death, Nero continued to use Locusta to eliminate threats, but the tides of power in Rome were beginning to shift. Nero's increasingly erratic behavior led to growing discontent among the Roman elite, and whispers of rebellion filled the air. Locusta, once a favored servant of the emperor, could feel the noose tightening around her neck. The very poison she had used to kill so many could one day be used against her.

The end for Locusta came with Nero's fall. In 68 AD, as Nero's enemies closed in and his reign collapsed, Locusta's fate was sealed. Without Nero's protection, she was left vulnerable to the vengeance of those she had wronged. After years of living in the shadows, dealing death with her poisons, Locusta was finally caught and brought to trial.

Unlike the poisons she had so carefully crafted, her death was not subtle. The Roman people, eager to see justice done, demanded a spectacle. Locusta was executed brutally, her body torn apart by wild beasts in the Colosseum—a fitting end for a woman whose life had been marked by death.

Locusta's story is a chilling reminder of the dangers of power, ambition, and knowledge used for destructive purposes. Her mastery of poisons, a skill that had once made her invaluable to emperors, became her undoing in the end. Her name has been remembered throughout history not as a healer or a wise herbalist, but as a symbol of the dark arts of death.

34. The Shadow

I n the heart of Czechoslovakia, during a time when the world was recovering from the upheavals of the 20th century, a figure emerged whose name would be spoken in fear and awe—Marie Fikáčková. Her story unfolded in the shadows of political instability and societal change, and her actions left an indelible mark on the nation.

Marie Fikáčková, born in the early 1920s, came from a modest family in a small village. The backdrop of her childhood was one of economic hardship, a time when Europe was still reeling from the effects of World War I and facing the looming uncertainty of the interwar period. Life was not easy, and young Marie learned early that survival required strength and cunning.

As a child, Marie was quiet, with a sharp mind that often went unnoticed in the chaos of rural life. Her parents, like many others in their village, struggled to make ends meet, and formal education was a luxury they couldn't fully afford. Despite her lack of schooling, Marie had a natural intelligence and an independent streak that would define her future.

Growing up in Czechoslovakia during a period of political turbulence meant that Marie was constantly exposed to a world of shifting ideologies and the growing tensions of the impending war. She absorbed the unrest around her, her mind shaped by the struggles of her family and the hardships of her community.

Marie's family life was shrouded in mystery, much like her later years. Few details remain about her upbringing or her relationships with her parents and siblings. What is clear is that the sense of familial warmth that usually shapes one's early years was absent. Perhaps it was this void that later fueled her ambition and her willingness to venture into the world of crime.

By the time Marie reached adulthood, the winds of war had once again swept through Europe. The devastation of World War II and the subsequent political upheavals in Czechoslovakia left the country in a fragile state, and Marie, like many others, found herself navigating a world in disarray. But unlike the ordinary citizens who sought stability, Marie thrived in the chaos.

Her entry into the world of crime wasn't immediate but was rather a gradual descent into the underworld. At first, she found herself drawn into small, petty crimes—minor thefts and scams that barely registered on the radar of law enforcement. But her ambitions were larger, and she knew she needed to carve out a more significant role in the world of organized crime if she wanted to escape the mundane life she had been born into.

The early years of her criminal career were dangerous. Marie was no stranger to risk, and she quickly learned how to navigate the treacherous web of Czechoslovakian society. In the shadows of Prague's alleys, she forged alliances with powerful figures in the criminal underworld, individuals who recognized her sharp mind and her ruthless determination. These alliances provided her with the protection and resources she needed to rise through the ranks.

Marie's first significant criminal act was a daring heist, one that would go down in Czech folklore for its audacity. Alongside her accomplices, she orchestrated the theft of valuable artifacts, outsmarting authorities and earning herself a reputation as a cunning and dangerous figure. This was just the beginning of her ascent into infamy.

As her reputation grew, so did her involvement in darker and more dangerous activities. Marie became embroiled in a series of high-profile assassinations, each one more meticulously planned than the last. Her victims were often political figures or rivals in the criminal underworld, and her ability to evade capture only added to her mystique.

The turning point in her life came when she orchestrated a particularly shocking murder—one that shook the very foundations of Czechoslovakian society. The details of the crime remain shrouded in secrecy, but it was clear that Marie had become a force to be reckoned with. Her rise to power was swift, and soon her name was whispered in fear across the nation.

Marie's methods were brutal, but they were also precise. She had an almost scientific approach to her crimes, planning every detail to ensure that her tracks were covered. Her ability to manipulate those around her, combined with her deep understanding of human psychology, made her an incredibly dangerous adversary.

But with power came enemies. Marie's rise to the top of the criminal world didn't go unnoticed, and soon she found herself the target of both law enforcement and rival gangs. Her ability to stay one step ahead of her pursuers was nothing short of remarkable, and for years she evaded capture, becoming a living legend in the process.

Despite her infamy, Marie remained elusive, her true motivations and character hidden behind a veil of secrecy. Those who encountered her described a woman of steely resolve, someone who seemed untouched by the moral qualms that governed most people's lives. Her eyes, they said, held a coldness that sent shivers down the spines of even the most hardened criminals.

Yet, beneath her calculated exterior, there was a complexity to Marie that few understood. Her life was one of constant conflict between her desire for power and the ever-present fear of betrayal. In the quiet moments, away from the violence and the chaos, one wonders if she ever questioned the path she had chosen. Did she feel guilt for the lives she had taken, or was her heart too hardened by the years of crime and survival?

As her notoriety grew, so did the public's fascination with her. Stories about Marie Fikáčková spread like wildfire, each tale more outlandish than the last. Some said she had sold her soul for power, while others claimed she was merely a product of the harsh world she had been born into. Whatever the truth, Marie had become a symbol—a figure who represented both the allure and the danger of unchecked ambition.

Her reign of terror eventually came to an end, but not without a final act of defiance. Marie was captured by authorities in a dramatic showdown, her arrest sending shockwaves through the country. The trial that followed was a spectacle, with the nation hanging on every detail of her crimes. But even in the face of justice, Marie remained defiant, never showing remorse for her actions.

Marie Fikáčková's legacy is one of enduring infamy. Her story continues to captivate those who are drawn to the darker side of human nature, and her name remains etched in the annals of Czechoslovakian crime. She was a woman who defied convention, who rose from nothing to become one of the most feared and notorious figures in the country's history.

In the end, Marie's life serves as a cautionary tale—a reminder of the thin line between ambition and destruction, between power and corruption. She was a woman of contradictions, capable of both brilliance and cruelty, and her story will continue to haunt those who dare to explore the shadows of human nature.

35. The Hidden Struggles

In the quiet corners of small-town Alabama, where the southern sun warms the streets and neighbors know each other by name, Martha Ann Johnson's story began. Her life, outwardly ordinary, concealed depths of pain, desperation, and darkness that would later shock the nation.

Born on October 6, 1955, Martha grew up as the youngest of three children in a modest household. Her family struggled financially, as her father was often absent due to work, leaving her mother to carry the weight of the household alone. Martha, a quiet and introspective child, sought solace in books, often disappearing into the worlds created by the stories she read. Yet, the warmth of her childhood was shadowed by instability, leaving emotional scars that would later influence her tragic decisions.

Martha's academic performance was average, though her teachers noticed her creativity. She excelled in writing and had dreams of becoming something more than her surroundings seemed to offer. But life, as it often does, took her in a different direction.

At the age of 18, Martha married Carl Johnson, a local mechanic. Their early years together were marked by struggle, as Carl's temper and the pressures of financial instability created cracks in their marriage. The couple had three children—Diane, Jennifer, and James. Martha loved her children dearly, but the pressures of motherhood, especially within the confines of a volatile marriage, weighed heavily on her.

Martha found moments of peace in her hobbies. Gardening became her escape, and neighbors often commented on the beauty of her flowers. She also loved to cook, and her dishes were a source of pride, something she could control in an otherwise unpredictable life. Despite the appearance of a dedicated homemaker, Martha's mental health was unraveling.

The birth of her third child, James, marked a turning point in Martha's life. She began to experience severe bouts of postpartum depression, a condition that went unnoticed and untreated. Depression began to consume her, amplifying the stresses of her marriage, financial difficulties, and the overwhelming responsibility of raising three children in a home fraught with tension. Carl's abusive behavior only deepened Martha's sense of hopelessness. The weight of her world bore down on her fragile mental state.

Despite her inner turmoil, Martha continued to present a facade of normalcy. She worked part-time to help supplement the family's income and tried to maintain stability for her children. But as her mental health continued to deteriorate, the once-loving mother began to view the world through a haze of depression, anxiety, and despair.

It was during these dark years that tragedy struck. Between 1980 and 1985, three of Martha's children—Diane, Jennifer, and James—died under suspicious circumstances. Each death was initially attributed to natural causes, and no one could imagine that the mother grieving at each funeral was hiding a terrible secret.

For years, Martha managed to hide the truth. But as with many secrets, the weight of it began to surface. A tip-off eventually led authorities to reopen the investigations into the children's deaths. What they discovered horrified the nation. Martha had been responsible for the deaths of her own children, driven by an overwhelming sense of despair and the crushing pressures of her life.

During her trial, the layers of Martha's mental state were laid bare. She was not a cold, calculating murderer, but a woman deeply troubled, a victim of her own untreated mental illness and the circumstances that had spiraled out of control. Psychiatric evaluations revealed the extent of her depression and the devastating impact it had on her ability to cope with the realities of her life. Her actions were monstrous, but they were also the product of a profound psychological collapse.

The revelations of Martha's crimes sparked outrage across the nation. How could a mother do such a thing? How had the system failed to notice the warning signs? As her story unfolded in the courtroom, it became clear that Martha's case was not just one of maternal betrayal, but a tragic example of the dangers of untreated mental illness, especially in a society that often overlooked the struggles of women in troubled domestic situations.

Martha Ann Johnson's case led to important discussions about mental health, maternal instincts, and the fragility of the human mind under extreme stress. Her actions were unforgivable, yet they underscored a desperate need for more mental health support for mothers and families facing similar challenges. Community outreach programs were established in the wake of her trial, aiming to provide support for struggling families, raising awareness about postpartum depression, and creating a safety net for those who might otherwise slip through the cracks.

Martha, herself, was a tragic figure—someone who could have been helped if the right resources and interventions had been available. But instead, she became a cautionary tale, a reminder of how untreated mental illness can lead to unimaginable consequences.

In the aftermath of her conviction, Martha's legacy remained one of sorrow and confusion. How could a woman who loved her children, who took pride in her home and garden, be capable of such horrific acts? The complexity of her story defied easy explanations, leaving many to grapple with the uncomfortable reality that human behavior is often shaped by forces beyond simple comprehension.

In her quieter moments, Martha likely wrestled with the enormity of what she had done. It's impossible to know what went through her mind as she cared for her children, knowing that she was also the cause of their deaths. Did she feel remorse? Guilt? Or was her mind too fractured by depression to fully grasp the magnitude of her actions? These are questions that remain unanswered.

Martha's trial ended with her being sentenced to life in prison. She would never again walk free, her life defined by the choices she made in her darkest moments. Yet, even behind bars, her story continued to reverberate, influencing changes in how society approached issues of child protection, mental health, and domestic violence.

Martha Ann Johnson's life, though marred by tragedy, forces us to confront difficult truths about the fragility of the human psyche. Her crimes were shocking, but they were also a reflection of deeper, systemic failures. She was a woman broken by her circumstances, driven to desperate measures by forces she could not control.

Today, Martha's name is remembered not just for her crimes, but as a reminder of the importance of mental health care, especially for mothers and families in distress. Her story challenges us to look beyond the surface and to understand the complexities of human behavior, mental illness, and the need for empathy in addressing the struggles that many face behind closed doors.

The story of Martha Ann Johnson is a somber reflection on the fragility of life and the devastating consequences of untreated mental illness. While her actions are unforgettable, they serve as a critical reminder that every life, no matter how ordinary it seems, can be touched by tragedy when the right support is absent.

36. The Shadowy Past

In the shadowed streets of Victorian England, where the industrial smog hung thick in the air and life for the poor was a relentless struggle, the name Mary Ann Cotton would soon become one whispered with fear. A name that symbolized the darkest side of human nature, hidden beneath the facade of an ordinary woman. Her story, wrapped in layers of deceit, desperation, and cold ambition, would later reveal her as one of Britain's most prolific female killers.

Mary Ann Cotton was born Mary Ann Robson on October 31, 1832, in a small, coal-mining village in County Durham, England. The daughter of Michael and Margaret Robson, her early life was filled with hardship. Like many families in the area, her father worked as a miner, spending long hours in dangerous conditions. The constant struggle for survival was etched into Mary Ann from an early age. Poverty and the harsh realities of a laborer's life in Victorian England defined her childhood, leaving a mark on her psyche that would later drive her to unspeakable acts.

She learned quickly that life was fragile. Her father's sudden death in a mining accident, when Mary Ann was only eight, devastated the family. This event would set the tone for her outlook on life—loss, survival, and the means to an end. The loss of her father forced her to mature quickly, and she was soon helping her mother around the house and caring for her siblings. Formal education was a luxury she could not afford, and instead, she grew adept at the practical skills necessary to run a household. But something darker simmered beneath the surface—a growing resentment, a desire for more than her bleak future promised.

At the age of 20, Mary Ann married William Mowbray, a miner, much like her father. Together, they had several children, but a disturbing pattern emerged. Child after child died in infancy, with their deaths attributed to various illnesses common at the time. Typhus, dysentery, and fever were frequent explanations for the loss of young lives in the squalor of Victorian slums. Yet, the sheer number of deaths surrounding Mary Ann began to raise quiet suspicions, though no one dared voice them.

Mourning became a familiar state for Mary Ann, though many in the village noticed how her grief seemed almost calculated. She always made sure to claim life insurance payouts for her children and husbands. What others couldn't see was the cold logic behind her actions—each death brought a small sum of money, just enough to keep her afloat in the cruel world she lived in.

After William Mowbray's sudden death in 1865 from what doctors described as a "gastric illness," Mary Ann collected life insurance and swiftly remarried George Ward, a local laborer. George, too, would soon fall ill and die under suspiciously similar circumstances. Gastrointestinal issues and stomach pains plagued him until he died in 1866. Mary Ann wept at his funeral, a widow once again, and collected yet another life insurance policy.

At this point, Mary Ann had mastered the art of blending in. She appeared the grieving wife and mother, always mourning the loss of another loved one. But with each death, she grew bolder. After her third marriage to James Robinson, a widower, Mary Ann's pattern continued. His children from a previous marriage began to fall ill and die, just like her own. One by one, they succumbed to strange illnesses that no doctor could definitively explain.

Mary Ann's charm and practical homemaking skills masked the truth behind her cold, calculated murders. She was able to maintain an air of normalcy, even as those around her continued to die. She moved through life with a chilling determination, caring for her surviving children with one hand and poisoning her husbands and stepchildren with the other.

Her fourth husband, Frederick Cotton, fared no better. Frederick, his two sons, and even his sister all died of mysterious illnesses. By now, people in the small villages were whispering, questioning the sheer number of deaths that seemed to follow Mary Ann. It was too many to ignore, too frequent to be mere bad luck.

The turning point came when her stepson, Charles Edward Cotton, died unexpectedly in 1872. This time, local authorities took notice. When a post-mortem examination revealed traces of arsenic in Charles's body, the pieces of Mary Ann's macabre puzzle began to fall into place. Authorities exhumed the bodies of several of her other victims, and arsenic was found in each. It became clear that Mary Ann had been methodically poisoning her victims, using arsenic to create what appeared to be natural deaths.

When Mary Ann Cotton was finally arrested, the public was horrified. Victorian society was shaken by the thought that a woman, especially a mother, could commit such atrocities. Her trial in 1873 captivated the nation. Here was a woman who had used the trust and intimacy of family life as a weapon. The press dubbed her "The Black Widow," and stories of her crimes spread far and wide.

During the trial, Mary Ann remained calm, steadfastly denying the charges. She portrayed herself as a victim of circumstance, a grieving mother and widow who had simply suffered more than her share of bad luck. But the evidence was overwhelming. Witnesses testified about her life insurance claims, the sudden deaths of her husbands and children, and the tell-tale symptoms of arsenic poisoning. The jury took less than an hour to convict her.

In her final days, Mary Ann showed little remorse. She maintained her innocence even as she faced the gallows. Her cold demeanor during her execution left many wondering if she was capable of feeling any guilt at all. On March 24, 1873, Mary Ann Cotton was hanged for the murder of her stepson Charles Edward Cotton. It was believed that she was responsible for the deaths of at least 21 people, though some estimates put the number even higher.

The case of Mary Ann Cotton left a lasting impact on Victorian England. It exposed the vulnerabilities of domestic life, where poison could be administered in the most intimate settings—through food, drink, and medicine. Her crimes led to a heightened awareness of the dangers of covert domestic violence and poison, and they paved the way for advancements in forensic science, particularly in the detection of arsenic.

Mary Ann Cotton's story remains a chilling reminder of the darkness that can lurk behind closed doors. She was a woman driven by greed, willing to sacrifice anyone, even her own children, to escape poverty and hardship. Her life is a testament to the extremes of human ambition and the depths of moral depravity.

"I never suspected she was capable of such cruelty. She seemed like a caring mother," one neighbor had said, reflecting the sentiments of many who had been fooled by Mary Ann's outward appearance of normalcy.

In the end, Mary Ann Cotton's legacy is not one of greatness but of horror. She stands as a reminder that evil can wear many masks—sometimes even that of a mother, tending to her children in the foggy, quiet streets of Victorian England.

37. The Tragic Legacy

In the wake of World War II, as Japan struggled to rebuild its shattered economy and society, a dark and tragic story emerged that would forever haunt the nation. Miyuki Ishikawa, once a trusted midwife, became the center of one of the most chilling criminal cases in Japanese history. Her actions, wrapped in secrecy and justified by a twisted sense of morality, would lead to the deaths of dozens of innocent infants and expose deep flaws in Japan's healthcare and social welfare systems.

Miyuki Ishikawa was born on January 24, 1897, in a small rural village in Japan, where tradition held strong and modernization was just beginning to sweep through the country. Growing up in a typical Japanese household, Miyuki's early life was shaped by the values of duty, respect, and resilience. Her childhood is largely undocumented, but like many girls in rural Japan at the time, her education would have been minimal, focused more on domestic responsibilities than formal schooling.

From an early age, Miyuki showed a strong will, an unflinching dedication to those around her, and a natural talent for caregiving. This sense of duty would lead her to pursue a career in midwifery—a field where compassion and skill were necessary to help guide new life into the world. It was here, in the shadows of maternity wards and struggling hospitals, that her dark journey began.

Miyuki married Takeshi Ishikawa, a medical practitioner, and together they settled into a life centered around their work in the healthcare sector. Takeshi's work as a doctor and Miyuki's reputation as a skilled midwife allowed them to build trust in their community, where the needs of mothers and newborns were often dire. Post-war Japan was a place of poverty and desperation, and many families struggled to care for the babies they brought into the world. Miyuki found herself facing these heartbreaking situations day after day.

The turning point in Miyuki's life came when she began to believe that she was helping these families by preventing the birth of children they couldn't afford to care for. The overcrowded hospitals and lack of social welfare support weighed heavily on her. Faced with the reality of families unable to provide for their infants, Miyuki made a decision that would lead to her infamous downfall—she began neglecting the care of newborns, allowing them to die through what she later called "mercy killings."

In the late 1940s, Miyuki's methods became darker and more deliberate. She believed she was sparing these children from a life of poverty and suffering, but in truth, she had crossed a line that no caregiver should ever cross. What started as neglect soon turned into systematic abandonment. The newborns were often left without the proper care or sustenance, resulting in their tragic deaths.

For years, the deaths went unnoticed or were brushed aside by authorities who were overwhelmed by the post-war chaos. After all, infant mortality was not uncommon in a country still reeling from the devastation of war. But as the number of dead infants under Miyuki's care began to rise, whispers of suspicion grew louder.

By the early 1950s, the authorities could no longer ignore the alarming pattern. An investigation was launched after one too many infants died under suspicious circumstances at the hospital where Miyuki worked. When investigators looked deeper, they uncovered a chilling truth: Miyuki Ishikawa had been directly responsible for the deaths of over 100 infants. The nation was stunned.

Miyuki was arrested, and her trial became a national sensation. In the courtroom, she appeared calm and composed, maintaining her belief that her actions had been acts of mercy. She argued that the state had failed these children by not providing adequate support for their parents and that she had merely done what she thought was necessary. To Miyuki, the overcrowded orphanages and the dire poverty that awaited these babies were far worse than the death she had delivered.

But the court saw things differently. The public, too, was horrified by the callousness of her actions. Miyuki's trial exposed not only her individual crimes but also the larger systemic failures that had allowed such atrocities to occur. The lack of social welfare, the failure of the healthcare system to support the most vulnerable, and the moral responsibility of caregivers became the central themes of the trial. People began to ask: How could such a thing happen? And more importantly, how could it be prevented from happening again?

As witnesses took the stand, the extent of Miyuki's actions became clear. Testimonies from nurses and hospital staff painted a picture of a woman who had grown desensitized to the suffering she caused. She had lost sight of the very oath she had taken as a midwife—to protect life at all costs. Instead, she had taken it upon herself to decide which lives were worth living. Her mental state, once compassionate and determined, had been consumed by a twisted logic that allowed her to justify her crimes.

Miyuki Ishikawa was eventually convicted of multiple counts of murder. She was sentenced to four years in prison—a sentence that many considered far too lenient given the gravity of her crimes. The verdict was met with outrage by the public, who saw her as the embodiment of cold, calculated cruelty. To this day, her name is synonymous with one of Japan's darkest chapters.

But Miyuki's story did not end with her imprisonment. Her case became a catalyst for widespread reforms in Japan's child welfare and healthcare systems. The Ishikawa Incident, as it came to be known, forced the government to take a hard look at how it cared for its most vulnerable citizens. Hospitals were given stricter guidelines for reporting infant deaths, social services were expanded to offer more support for struggling families, and new laws were introduced to ensure that cases like this would never happen again.

In the years following her release from prison, Miyuki faded into obscurity. She never publicly expressed remorse for her actions, and the true motivations behind her decisions remain a matter of speculation. Some argue that she was a victim of the system—overwhelmed by the impossible pressures placed on her as a caregiver in a country still healing from war. Others believe she was a cold-blooded murderer, driven by a twisted sense of power over life and death.

Miyuki's case continues to be studied by criminologists, psychologists, and historians as an example of how systemic failures can lead to personal tragedies. It is a story that reminds us of the thin line between compassion and cruelty, and the devastating consequences when that line is crossed.

Today, Miyuki Ishikawa's legacy lives on, not as a figure of greatness, but as a cautionary tale. Her name serves as a reminder of the profound responsibilities that caregivers bear and the importance of ensuring that those who care for the vulnerable are themselves supported and held accountable.

"She seemed kind and caring, but we never imagined the horrors happening under her watch," one of her former colleagues remarked during the trial. The community that had once trusted Miyuki with their newborns was left grappling with the painful truth of her betrayal.

Miyuki's story forces us to confront uncomfortable questions about the nature of caregiving, the pressures faced by those in positions of power, and the systemic failures that can allow such tragedies to occur. It is a story that resonates even today, as societies continue to grapple with issues of healthcare, social responsibility, and the ethical boundaries of caregiving.

In recounting the life of Miyuki Ishikawa, we are reminded that the path to tragedy is often paved with good intentions gone horribly wrong. Her actions, while inexcusable, reflect the deep flaws in a system that failed both her and the countless children who lost their lives under her care.

38. The Depths of Depravity

I n the grey streets of post-war Manchester, where the industrial heart of England beat amidst smoke-filled skies and struggling communities, the story of Myra Hindley began. Born on July 23, 1942, she seemed like any other child in the working-class neighborhoods—unremarkable, quiet, and largely unnoticed. But behind that facade, Myra's life would spiral into one of the darkest chapters in British history.

Myra was the eldest of two children. Her father, Bob Hindley, served in the military during World War II and was often absent from the family home. When he returned, the scars of war left him stern and emotionally distant. Her mother, Nellie, struggled to provide for the family, and the weight of raising two children under economic hardship became overwhelming. It was a household where love was scarce, and Myra learned early on to fend for herself.

Growing up in a tough, post-war world, Myra's childhood was filled with instability. The school provided little escape. She was described as an average student, but she faced bullying, and her tough exterior began to form. The instability in her home and school life made her crave acceptance, and it was this vulnerability that would later be manipulated.

By her teenage years, Myra began to change. She dyed her hair blonde, wore more provocative clothing, and started seeking out ways to stand out from the crowd. Despite the tough persona she built, inside Myra was a confused young woman, desperate for approval, for a purpose.

At 18, she began working clerical jobs, and it was during one of these jobs that she met Ian Brady, a man who would change the course of her life—and the lives of many others—in ways no one could have imagined. Ian was quiet, intense, and intelligent. He was different from anyone Myra had ever met, and she was instantly drawn to him. But there was something darker about Ian. He was fascinated by the atrocities of the Nazis, by crime, by violence, and he fed these ideas to Myra. Slowly, he began to mold her thoughts and her beliefs, until she shared his disturbing worldview.

Their relationship became toxic. Ian was charismatic and domineering, and Myra followed him into a world of fantasy and violence. Together, they began to fantasize about committing crimes, about taking control in the most brutal way possible—through murder. Myra's need for acceptance was so deep that she went along with Ian's escalating sadistic fantasies, her own moral compass buried beneath her obsession with him.

Their first victim was 16-year-old Pauline Reade. It was July 12, 1963, when Myra, with her blonde hair and seemingly kind smile, lured Pauline into her van, asking for help finding a missing glove. Pauline, trusting this older girl, climbed in, unaware that Ian Brady was waiting nearby. Once they reached the desolate moors outside Manchester, Ian attacked and killed Pauline while Myra watched, doing nothing to stop him. In fact, she later helped bury the body. This first murder set them on a horrific path that would span two years and claim the lives of four more children.

Each of their victims—John Kilbride, Keith Bennett, Lesley Ann Downey, and Edward Evans—were young, innocent, and unsuspecting. Myra would use her appearance to gain their trust, convincing them to get into her car with promises of a ride or help. Once they were isolated on the moors, Ian would strike. The pair took pleasure in tormenting their victims, recording some of their brutal acts on tape.

The sheer cruelty of their crimes shocked the nation. They didn't just kill their victims; they tortured them, making sure to record their last moments of terror. One of the most heartbreaking details of the case was the recording of 10-year-old Lesley Ann Downey, where her cries for her mother were captured in chilling detail.

As their crimes escalated, so did their sense of invincibility. But it was their final victim, 17-year-old Edward Evans, that would lead to their capture. Unlike their previous murders, this one was witnessed by Myra's brother-in-law, David Smith, who had been invited to watch the killing. Horrified by what he saw, Smith contacted the police the next day, and on October 7, 1965, Myra and Ian were arrested.

The trial that followed captured the nation. Myra, with her striking blonde hair, became the symbol of evil femininity—a woman who had aided in the sadistic murders of innocent children. Ian was already seen as a monster, but for many, it was harder to understand how Myra could have participated. She appeared calm and composed throughout the trial, showing little emotion as the horrific details of their crimes were revealed.

"Myra was just as guilty as Ian," one of the detectives later said. "Her calm demeanor in court was chilling. There was no remorse, no regret."

The nation was horrified as the evidence mounted. Recordings of Lesley Ann Downey's final moments were played in court, and both Ian and Myra were convicted of murder. Myra received two life sentences, and she would spend the rest of her life in prison. Despite several attempts to gain parole, public outcry ensured that she would never be released.

Even in prison, Myra remained a subject of fascination and revulsion. Over the years, she tried to distance herself from Ian, portraying herself as a victim of his manipulation. She claimed that he had controlled her every move, that she had been powerless to stop him. But few believed her. Her role in the murders was too active, too calculated, to be dismissed as mere influence. The tapes, the evidence of her luring the children, and her cold detachment during the crimes left no doubt of her complicity.

"Myra's eyes," a police officer who had been involved in the investigation recalled, "there was something dark in them, something that chilled you to the bone."

In the years following her imprisonment, Myra became a symbol of the darkest aspects of human nature—proof that even those who seem ordinary, those who appear harmless, can be capable of unimaginable evil. Her case raised countless questions about the nature of evil, about how someone like Myra, who had once been an innocent child herself, could become involved in such horrific acts.

Her story challenges us to confront uncomfortable truths: How much of her actions were a result of Ian Brady's influence? Could she have ever been saved, or was she always capable of such cruelty? These questions linger, unanswered.

Myra Hindley's life ended in 2002, after 36 years in prison. She died without ever fully explaining or taking responsibility for her role in the Moors Murders. Her death closed the book on one of the most infamous criminal cases in British history, but the scars she and Ian Brady left on the nation—and on the families of their victims—remain.

For the families of Pauline, John, Keith, Lesley Ann, and Edward, the pain never fully healed. Keith Bennett's body was never found, and his mother died never knowing where her son was buried, a heartbreaking reminder of the cruelty of Hindley and Brady's actions.

"Myra Hindley took more than just the lives of those children," one of the victim's family members said. "She stole our peace, our futures, and left us with questions that can never be answered."

Myra Hindley's legacy is one of evil. Her life serves as a stark reminder that darkness can hide behind the most unassuming faces. She was not a monster in appearance, but her actions, and her willingness to participate in the torture and murder of children, reveal the true depth of her depravity.

In the end, Myra Hindley will always be remembered not for who she was, but for what she did—a haunting reminder of the fragility of innocence and the darkness that can sometimes lie within.

39. The Giggling Granny

I n the quiet, sun-dappled towns of mid-20th century America, a seemingly ordinary woman named Nannie Doss moved through life like any typical grandmother. Her smile was warm, her demeanor gentle, and her reputation for being a loving homemaker was solid. Yet behind that facade of domestic tranquility, Nannie harbored a deadly secret, one that would shock a nation and earn her the chilling moniker, "The Giggling Granny."

Nannie Doss was born as Nancy Hazle on November 4, 1905, in Blue Mountain, Alabama, into a world marked by hardship and struggle. Her father, James Hazle, was a stern and controlling man, often abusive, while her mother, Lou, was overwhelmed by the demands of keeping the family together. Nannie's childhood was rough, full of instability, and marred by the lack of affection from her parents. Poverty seeped into every aspect of their lives, and the small, rural town did little to provide any escape from the turmoil inside her home. Nannie, as the eldest of five siblings, was forced to help with the housework from a young age, rarely attending school.

She longed for love and happiness, something she would later describe as her greatest desire, though how she sought these things turned horrifying. Early on, Nannie dreamed of romantic love and the ideal life that she read about in the magazines she adored. But life for Nannie was anything but ideal. Her dreams were dashed by a strict father who refused to let her socialize with boys or live with the freedoms that many of her peers experienced.

By the age of 16, desperate to escape her oppressive home life, Nannie married for the first time. Her husband, Charley Braggs, was a quiet man who worked in a local factory. The couple had four children together in quick succession, and their home seemed to be a place of domestic bliss. However, beneath the surface, Nannie's marriage was fraught with problems. Charley was emotionally distant and often left Nannie to care for the children on her own, fueling a resentment that simmered under her cheerful exterior.

It wasn't long before tragedy struck. Two of their young children died suddenly under suspicious circumstances. Though the deaths were officially blamed on food poisoning, Charley suspected something darker. His suspicions were further fueled by Nannie's increasing reliance on alcohol and her erratic behavior. Soon after the children's deaths, Charley took their surviving children and fled, leaving Nannie behind.

Nannie's search for love didn't end there. She went on to marry four more times, and with each marriage came more death. Her husbands died mysteriously, one after another, from what appeared to be natural causes. Each time, Nannie was left with a small insurance payout, enough to keep her financially stable. She played the grieving widow with expert precision, earning sympathy from neighbors and friends who never suspected that the woman they knew could be capable of murder.

In reality, Nannie was using arsenic to poison her victims, carefully mixing it into their food and drinks. The methodical nature of her crimes was chilling. She often targeted those closest to her—her husbands, children, grandchildren, and even her mother. Each murder was calculated, and each death brought her a step closer to the romanticized life she believed she deserved.

Despite the trail of bodies left in her wake, Nannie managed to avoid suspicion for years. Her charm and outward kindness made it difficult for anyone to believe that she could be involved in such heinous acts. Even when she was finally caught, it wasn't the sheer number of deaths that gave her away but rather a mistake in covering her tracks. Her fifth and final husband, Samuel Doss, was a stern but seemingly kind man. Unlike her previous husbands, Samuel did not tolerate Nannie's whimsical nature and her obsession with romance novels. He was strict, and controlling, and did not allow Nannie to spend money frivolously.

Not long after their marriage, Samuel fell ill. Doctors initially thought it was severe digestive issues, but when he survived, Nannie tried again. This time, she slipped arsenic into his food. Samuel died soon after, and his doctor, suspicious of the rapid deterioration, ordered an autopsy. The results revealed large amounts of arsenic in Samuel's system, and Nannie was arrested.

Even as the investigation into the death of Samuel Doss revealed the shocking truth, Nannie maintained her calm, cheerful demeanor. When questioned by police, she laughed and smiled, even as she confessed to killing four of her husbands, her mother, her sister, her grandson, and her mother-in-law. Her chilling admissions were often accompanied by giggles, which earned her the macabre nickname "The Giggling Granny."

Her trial, which took place in 1955, captivated the nation. How could a grandmotherly figure with such a sweet smile be capable of such monstrous acts? How could someone who baked pies for her neighbors and tended to her garden with care be a serial killer? These questions haunted the American public, but for Nannie, the answers seemed simple.

"I was just tired of them," she said when asked why she had murdered so many people. For Nannie, the deaths were a means to an end—a way to escape unhappy marriages, financial struggles, and the responsibilities that came with family life. She had no qualms about using murder to carve out the life she felt she deserved.

The courtroom was stunned by her lack of remorse. Even as she faced the possibility of execution, Nannie never wavered from her cheerful, almost flippant demeanor. She seemed to see the trial as little more than a formality, something to be endured before moving on. The details of her crimes were horrifying, and yet Nannie displayed no signs of guilt or regret.

Her trial led to her conviction, and Nannie Doss was sentenced to life in prison. The judge chose not to seek the death penalty due to her age, but Nannie spent the rest of her life behind bars. Even in prison, she maintained her trademark smile, reportedly laughing and joking with her fellow inmates as if she had never committed a crime at all.

Despite the horrors she had inflicted on her family, Nannie became somewhat of a celebrity in prison. Her case continued to fascinate the public, and journalists visited her regularly, eager to get a glimpse of the infamous "Giggling Granny." She charmed them, as she had charmed so many before, with her polite manners and infectious laugh.

Nannie Doss died in prison in 1965, but her legacy endures as one of the most chilling examples of domestic violence in American history. Her case challenged the idea that murderers fit a particular mold—that they are angry, violent people who cannot hide their intentions. Nannie's crimes revealed that evil can wear a mask of normalcy, that it can be hidden behind a sweet smile and a warm laugh.

Nannie's story forces us to confront uncomfortable truths about the nature of evil. How could a woman so seemingly normal, so loving and maternal, commit such horrific acts? What drove her to kill not just once, but over and over again? Was it her upbringing, her failed marriages, or something darker that lay within her all along?

"I always thought she was such a kind woman," a neighbor once said, after Nannie's arrest. "She loved her garden, always brought over baked goods, and looked after her family. I can't believe it."

Nannie's legacy is a chilling reminder that sometimes, the greatest threats are those that come from within the home, from the people we trust the most. Her life and crimes have been studied by psychologists, criminal investigators, and historians, all seeking to understand what could drive a person to commit such unthinkable acts.

Ultimately, Nannie Doss's story is one of deception and death. Behind her laughter lay a woman who saw murder as a tool, who took the lives of those closest to her with little regard for their suffering. She remains a haunting figure, a reminder that evil does not always come in the form of a monster—it can wear the face of a smiling grandmother.

40. The Banality of Evil

Rosemary West, a woman whose crimes would come to symbolize the depths of human depravity, was born on November 29, 1953, in Northam, Devon. Her early years were filled with turbulence, as she grew up in a household marked by violence, abuse, and poverty. Her father, Bill Letts, was a strict and abusive man, his outbursts of anger were often directed at his wife, Daisy, and their children. Life in the Letts household was unstable, and it left its mark on young Rosemary, shaping her into someone who would later shock the world with her unimaginable cruelty.

Rosemary's school years were difficult. She struggled academically, finding it hard to concentrate amidst the chaos of her home life. Her relationship with her father was particularly complicated. Bill's violent tendencies often spilled over into controlling his daughter, and there were dark rumors about inappropriate behavior that further isolated Rosemary. In many ways, her childhood set the stage for the choices she would make later in life.

In the early 1970s, Rosemary met Fred West, a man whose own past was filled with violence and darkness. Fred was charismatic in his own way, though there was always something unsettling about him. He had already been involved in criminal activities, including theft and sexual assault. When he met Rosemary, they quickly formed a bond, both drawn to the darker sides of one another. Together, they would embark on a path of destruction that left an indelible scar on British history.

Fred and Rosemary married in 1972, and from the outside, they seemed like a relatively normal couple. They lived at 25 Cromwell Street, a nondescript house in Gloucester that would soon become notorious as the site of their horrific crimes. The West had several children, and their home, though chaotic, appeared outwardly normal. Neighbors would see Rosemary in the garden, tending to her plants or chatting amiably, never suspecting the horrors that were taking place behind closed doors.

But inside the walls of 25 Cromwell Street, Rosemary and Fred were running a house of horrors. Together, they abducted, tortured, sexually abused, and murdered young women. Many of the victims were lured in by the seemingly innocent couple, only to meet a tragic and brutal fate. Rosemary, who had by then become an active participant in the crimes, was often the one to lure the victims into their trap. Once inside, the victims were subjected to unimaginable torment before being killed and buried in the garden or cellar of their homes.

One of the most chilling aspects of Rosemary's participation was her role in the murder of her own daughter, Heather West. Heather had endured years of abuse at the hands of her parents, and when she became a threat to expose their crimes, Fred and Rosemary decided she had to be silenced. Heather's body was buried in the garden, along with many of their other victims. It was a crime that shocked even seasoned investigators.

The West's reign of terror went undetected for years. They were cunning, careful, and meticulous in hiding their crimes. The couple maintained a facade of normalcy, and Rosemary, in particular, appeared to be an ordinary, albeit troubled, housewife. She continued to raise her children, work menial jobs, and interact with neighbors as though nothing was amiss. To the outside world, Rosemary was just another mother trying to manage a large household. But inside, the reality was far darker.

It wasn't until 1994, when police began investigating the disappearance of Heather West, that the full extent of their crimes came to light. As investigators dug deeper, they uncovered the remains of several victims buried in the cellar and garden of 25 Cromwell Street. The discovery sent shockwaves through the nation. Fred and Rosemary were arrested, and what followed was one of the most notorious criminal investigations in UK history.

During the trial, details of the West's horrific acts emerged, painting a picture of unimaginable cruelty. The court heard how Rosemary had been an active participant in the sexual abuse and torture of the victims, working alongside Fred to carry out their sadistic desires. The evidence against them was overwhelming, yet throughout the trial, Rosemary maintained her innocence. She denied any involvement, even as witness after witness, and a piece of forensic evidence proved otherwise.

Her cold, detached demeanor during the trial stunned observers. Rosemary showed little emotion, even as the gruesome details of her crimes were laid bare. She offered no remorse, no explanation for the atrocities she had committed. Her lack of empathy, combined with the horrific nature of the crimes, made it difficult for the public to comprehend how someone could commit such acts and remain so indifferent.

Fred West never faced justice in court; he hanged himself in his prison cell before the trial could conclude. This left Rosemary to face the full brunt of the legal proceedings alone. In 1995, she was convicted of ten counts of murder and sentenced to life imprisonment without the possibility of parole. The judge described her crimes as "evil beyond belief," and the British public was left reeling from the revelations.

The case of Fred and Rosemary West highlighted not only the depths of human depravity but also the failings of the system to protect vulnerable people. Many of their victims were young women who had fallen through the cracks of society—runaways, drifters, or those living on the margins. The West preyed on these vulnerable individuals, exploiting their isolation and desperation.

In the aftermath of the case, there were calls for reforms in the way law enforcement handled missing persons cases, as well as improvements in social services to better identify at-risk individuals. The crimes also sparked a national conversation about domestic violence, abuse, and the hidden dangers that can lurk within seemingly ordinary families.

Rosemary West remains in prison to this day, a shadow of the woman who once terrified a nation. Her name is synonymous with evil, a symbol of the darkest aspects of the human soul. But even in prison, Rosemary has shown little remorse. She continues to maintain her innocence, despite the overwhelming evidence against her.

Those who knew her before her arrest still struggle to reconcile the woman they thought they knew with the monster she became. "She was always so polite," a neighbor recalled, still in disbelief. "You never would have guessed she was capable of such things."

The case of Rosemary West forces us to confront uncomfortable truths about the nature of evil. How could someone so seemingly normal, so ordinary, commit such extraordinary acts of cruelty? What drives a person to cross the line from abuse to murder? These are questions that psychologists, criminologists, and the public continue to grapple with.

In the end, the story of Rosemary West is not just about one woman's descent into darkness, but about the fragility of trust, the dangers of unchecked power, and the horrifying consequences of a life defined by violence and cruelty. The legacy of her crimes continues to haunt the families of the victims and the nation as a whole, a chilling reminder of the evil that can lurk behind even the most benign facades.

41. A Mother's Dark Path

Theresa Jimmie Cross, later known as Theresa Knorr, was born on March 14, 1946, in Sacramento, California. Her early years were clouded by poverty and instability. The third of Chester and Swannie Cross's children, Theresa grew up in a troubled home where emotional and financial support were scarce. Her father's frequent absences and her mother's struggles with mental illness created an environment of neglect that deeply shaped Theresa's perception of the world. From a young age, she was familiar with chaos and unpredictability, experiences that would later become defining forces in her life.

Theresa's education was inconsistent. Moving from one place to another, her schooling was interrupted, and she never really found her footing. With little guidance, her youth was spent mostly on survival rather than nurturing any talents or ambitions. Her relationships within the family were distant, and like many children in such unstable households, she grew up emotionally detached. The seeds of her future cruelty were unknowingly sown in the fractures of her early life.

Theresa married young and frequently. She had six children with multiple husbands, none of whom stayed for long. Each marriage ended either in divorce or separation, leaving her to manage her growing household by herself. It soon became clear that Theresa was not a nurturing mother. Instead, she exerted control over her children through manipulation, violence, and fear. What should have been a home filled with love and care was, instead, a house of terror for her children.

Her darkest actions began to unfold in the 1980s when she turned her children into prisoners of her cruelty. Theresa's mental state was deteriorating. She was paranoid, convinced that her children were conspiring against her. She believed that they needed to be punished, and in her mind, the punishments were justified. She began to focus her wrath, particularly on her two daughters, Suesan and Sheila. Her other children, terrified and powerless, could do nothing to stop her.

Theresa's paranoia about Suesan started when she accused her daughter of witchcraft. In her increasingly twisted worldview, she believed that Suesan had put a curse on her, and in Theresa's mind, the only way to fix the situation was to burn the evil out of her daughter. She locked Suesan in a room and deprived her of food for weeks. The violence escalated when she shot Suesan in the back, leaving her in excruciating pain. Instead of seeking medical attention, Theresa let her daughter suffer.

Finally, in an act of horrendous cruelty, Theresa forced her sons to help her dispose of Suesan's body. They were ordered to burn the remains in the desert, erasing any trace of their sister. The family's world was plunged into even deeper terror, with everyone trapped under the weight of Theresa's oppressive control.

Sheila, Theresa's other daughter, became the next victim. Theresa's hatred toward her children grew darker, and she soon turned her focus to Sheila, whom she accused of being promiscuous. In a bizarre twist, Theresa believed that Sheila's supposed promiscuity would disgrace the family, so she confined her to a small, airless closet for months, where she eventually died of starvation and neglect. Once again, Theresa ordered her sons to help dispose of the body, adding another layer of horror to their already tormented existence.

By the time law enforcement discovered the full extent of Theresa's crimes, it was clear that this was not just a case of maternal neglect—it was systematic torture and murder. Her manipulation and control over her children were so complete that even the surviving siblings were hesitant to speak out, their minds twisted by years of fear and obedience to their mother.

For years, Theresa managed to evade suspicion. She maintained a façade of normalcy, deceiving those around her into thinking she was just another struggling single mother. But beneath that mask was a narcissist driven by a need for absolute control, a woman whose cruelty knew no bounds. Neighbors saw her as a troubled woman, but none could have imagined the horrific reality unfolding behind closed doors.

Theresa's ability to maintain this illusion of normalcy is one of the most chilling aspects of her story. Despite the horrors her children endured, she outwardly appeared calm and composed. Her crimes went unnoticed by authorities for years because she manipulated those around her with such skill, keeping the abuse hidden from prying eyes.

The discovery of her crimes in 1993 shocked the nation. After years of torment and abuse, one of her surviving children, William, finally found the courage to come forward and reveal the truth to the police. His confession sparked an investigation that would bring to light the full extent of Theresa's atrocities. Authorities were horrified by what they uncovered: two of her children were dead, and the rest were left physically and emotionally scarred for life.

Theresa Knorr was arrested and brought to trial. The details of her crimes horrified the court. The public was appalled at the extent of the abuse, and the media quickly dubbed her one of the most monstrous mothers in American history. During the trial, Theresa showed little remorse. In fact, she maintained a chilling detachment throughout the proceedings, insisting that her actions were justified and that she was not to blame for the deaths of her children.

The trial exposed not only Theresa's cruelty but also the failure of the social system to protect her children. Despite clear signs of abuse and neglect, no one had intervened to stop her. The case sparked outrage and led to calls for reforms in child protection services. People questioned how such horrors could have gone unnoticed for so long, and it became a rallying point for those advocating for better safeguards for vulnerable children.

In 1995, Theresa Knorr was convicted of multiple counts of murder and sentenced to life in prison without the possibility of parole. Her children, who had lived in fear of their mother for so long, were finally free from her control. But the damage was done—the scars she left on their lives would never fully heal. The courtroom heard from William and Theresa's other surviving children, who spoke of the years of torment they had endured. Their stories painted a bleak picture of a household ruled by fear and brutality, where love and compassion had no place.

Theresa Knorr remains in prison, her name forever associated with some of the most horrific acts of maternal cruelty in American history. Her case stands as a dark reminder of the capacity for evil that can exist within families and the devastating consequences of unchecked violence and abuse. To this day, her legacy evokes horror and disbelief, a testament to the lives lost and the lives forever changed by her actions.

As one neighbor once said, "She seemed like a troubled woman, but no one could have imagined the extent of her cruelty."

Theresa Knorr's story challenges us to look deeper at the dynamics of abuse within families. It forces us to confront uncomfortable truths about the potential for evil within those we trust the most. How could a mother commit such heinous acts against her own children? How did the system fail to protect them? These are questions that still resonate today, as we grapple with the implications of her crimes and the lessons we can learn from them.

In the end, Theresa Knorr's life is not defined by the hardships she endured but by the atrocities she committed. Her story is a sobering reminder of the darkness that can exist within even the closest of family bonds and the importance of vigilance in protecting those who are most vulnerable.

42. The Hidden Danger

Tillie Klimek's life began far from the dark path she would later walk. Born as Tillie Gburek on September 18, 1876, in Poland, she grew up in a world of hardship. Political unrest and economic challenges defined her early years, shaping her into a resilient and resourceful woman. Like many others seeking a better life, she immigrated to the United States, where she would settle in the vibrant, yet gritty neighborhoods of Chicago. But what appeared to be the start of a new life was only the beginning of a chilling tale of murder and deception that would leave a mark on American criminal history.

Tillie was known in her community as a typical grandmotherly figure—quiet, unassuming, and kind. She appeared to live an ordinary life, tending to her domestic duties, chatting with neighbors, and baking in her small kitchen. But beneath this façade lay a calculating mind, one that saw family members not as loved ones, but as obstacles or opportunities for financial gain.

The early years of Tillie's life in America are largely undocumented, but she lived through the common struggles of an immigrant woman in early 20th-century Chicago. She married several times, and each of her marriages ended in tragedy. Her husbands, one by one, died under suspicious circumstances, and it seemed as though Tillie was cursed with bad luck. Yet, each time a husband died, Tillie was the recipient of life insurance payouts, a fact that should have raised suspicions sooner.

Her first husband, John Mitkiewicz, was the first to succumb to what Tillie claimed was a mysterious illness. At the time, no one suspected foul play. After all, John had been ill for some time, and death wasn't uncommon in those days. People thought Tillie was a devoted wife who had simply endured the heartbreak of losing her husband. She grieved publicly, but behind closed doors, her thoughts were cold and calculating. She had set the stage for what would become a deadly pattern.

Shortly after John's death, Tillie remarried. Her second husband, Joseph Ruskowski, would soon follow the same fate as John. Again, there was no reason to question the unfortunate turn of events. Illness swept through neighborhoods frequently, and families often lost loved ones unexpectedly.

Tillie, once again, collected life insurance money, keeping her calm demeanor intact as she continued her daily life. Neighbors, unaware of the tragedy unfolding, saw her as a devoted and grieving widow, but Tillie's heart had long since frozen to any semblance of compassion.

Tillie's third husband, Frank Kupczyk, was different. He lived longer, and by this time, Tillie had developed a certain confidence in her murderous abilities. Poison became her weapon of choice, a slow and silent killer that left little evidence in its wake. She prepared meals laced with arsenic, watching as Frank's health began to deteriorate. Neighbors noticed that Tillie had an eerie talent for predicting deaths. She would often tell her friends that she had a dream that her husband would die soon, and in time, her "predictions" always came true.

When Frank finally succumbed to the poison, Tillie didn't mourn. Instead, she celebrated privately, feeling a sense of satisfaction in her control over life and death. But her murderous spree didn't stop with her husbands. Tillie soon turned her attention to stepchildren and other family members. Anyone who stood in her way or became an inconvenience found themselves becoming part of her deadly plan. She was ruthless, and her desire for financial gain and control over those around her became insatiable.

Tillie's mental state during these years is a matter of speculation, but it's clear that her mind has become twisted by greed and a deep lack of empathy. She viewed her victims not as people but as pawns in her game. Each death was a calculated move, and the financial gains were her reward. Yet, she hid her true nature behind the mask of a caring wife and mother, a woman who, outwardly, seemed to fit neatly into the role society expected of her.

Her manipulation extended far beyond her victims. Tillie was skilled at deceiving those around her. She charmed neighbors, played the grieving widow convincingly, and kept a veneer of normalcy even as the bodies piled up. Her ability to compartmentalize her crimes from her public persona is one of the most chilling aspects of her story. To her friends, Tillie was just another woman struggling through life's challenges—no one could have imagined the dark secret she harbored.

It was only after the death of her fourth husband, Joseph Klimek, that authorities began to grow suspicious. Joseph had fallen ill like Tillie's previous husbands, but this time, his family intervened. His symptoms of poisoning had become too obvious to ignore, and they demanded an investigation. Tillie's world of deception began to crumble as investigators dug deeper into her past.

The autopsies of her previous husbands revealed traces of arsenic, a discovery that would seal Tillie's fate. Neighbors who once sympathized with her began to piece together the unsettling truth. Tillie's so-called "gift" of predicting deaths wasn't a gift at all—it was a confession of her crimes, hidden in plain sight.

During her trial, the public was captivated by the story of the "Giggling Granny," a nickname that belied the horror of her actions. Tillie remained defiant, maintaining her innocence despite the overwhelming evidence against her. Her lack of remorse shocked the courtroom, as did her cold demeanor when discussing the deaths of her loved ones. She seemed more concerned with how she was perceived than with the lives she had taken.

"I didn't do it," she insisted time and again, but the poison in her victims' bodies told a different story.

Her trial revealed the extent of her cruelty and manipulation, and the public was left to grapple with the question of how such evil could hide behind such a seemingly normal façade. Tillie had used the trust and intimacy of familial relationships to carry out her murders, exploiting the very bonds that should have protected her victims.

In the end, Tillie Klimek was sentenced to life in prison, where she spent the rest of her days. Her case remains a cautionary tale about the dangers that can lurk behind closed doors, about the capacity for evil within seemingly ordinary people. Tillie's legacy is one of horror and disbelief, a reminder that appearances can be deceiving and that trust, once broken, can have deadly consequences.

The story of Tillie Klimek forces us to confront uncomfortable truths about the nature of evil and the fragility of human relationships. She was a woman who, by all outward appearances, should have been a loving wife, mother, and grandmother. Instead, she was a cold-blooded killer, driven by greed and jealousy, willing to destroy those closest to her for personal gain.

Tillie's crimes left a deep scar on her community, and her name remains synonymous with betrayal and cruelty. Her ability to deceive those around her, to hide her true nature behind a mask of kindness, is what makes her story so chilling. It's a reminder that the darkest evils often come from those we least expect and that sometimes, the most dangerous place is the one we call home.

43. The Poisonous Obsession

V era Renczi was the kind of woman who drew people in. Born on July 5, 1903, in Bucharest, Romania, her charm and beauty were undeniable. With dark eyes that seemed to conceal secrets and a soft, cultured voice, she had the air of someone who had experienced too much too soon. Growing up in a middle-class family, Vera had an upbringing that, on the surface, seemed quite ordinary. Nothing about her early life hinted at the darkness that would later consume her.

From a young age, Vera was intelligent and introspective. She enjoyed poetry and literature, often losing herself in romantic stories. But those romantic ideals would later twist into something sinister. What Vera longed for wasn't just love—it was control. The idea of anyone leaving her, of a relationship ending, or of someone betraying her, was unbearable. She didn't just want to be loved; she wanted to possess. That possessiveness would eventually lead her down a path of unimaginable cruelty.

Vera's first marriage came in her early twenties. She was beautiful, well-read, and graceful—everything a man could want in a wife. Her first husband, a wealthy businessman, seemed like the perfect match. But Vera's jealousy quickly surfaced. She became suspicious of his every move, convinced he was unfaithful. To others, they appeared to be the perfect couple, but behind closed doors, Vera's mind was unraveling.

It wasn't long before her husband fell ill. Doctors couldn't figure out what was wrong with him—he seemed healthy, but his condition worsened day by day. Within months, he was dead, and Vera was a widow. She grieved publicly, shedding tears at the funeral, playing the part of the heartbroken wife. No one suspected her of foul play. But Vera had a secret: she had poisoned him, unable to bear the thought of him leaving her for another woman. In her mind, it was better that he die loving her than live and betray her.

Vera remarried soon after her first husband's death. Her new husband, another wealthy man, was completely unaware of the fate that awaited him. Like her first husband, he quickly became the target of Vera's controlling behavior. She monitored his every move, questioning him constantly, her paranoia growing more intense. When he began spending more time away from home, Vera's fears turned into fury. She couldn't stand the thought of him leaving her, and so, she poisoned him too.

But Vera's string of murders didn't stop there. Over the years, she married several times, and each husband met the same fate. Her weapon of choice was arsenic, a poison that worked slowly and quietly, allowing her to maintain her façade of innocence. Each time a husband died, Vera played the grieving widow, and each time, no one suspected her. She was too beautiful, too refined—how could such a delicate woman be capable of murder?

Vera's son, who had been born from a previous relationship, was the one person she seemed to truly love. But even that love was tainted by her possessiveness. As her son grew older, Vera's fear of losing him to another woman grew. She became controlling, keeping a tight grip on his life, desperate to keep him close. When he eventually began to date, Vera couldn't handle it. She felt betrayed as if her own son was abandoning her. In a final, desperate act of control, she poisoned him too.

By the time authorities finally began to suspect Vera, it was too late for many of her victims. Neighbors had started to whisper about the strange number of deaths surrounding her, but it wasn't until the bodies of her husbands and her son were found buried in her garden that the truth came to light. Vera was arrested, and the public was horrified as the details of her crimes emerged.

During her trial, Vera remained calm, even cold. She showed no remorse, no sign that she regretted what she had done. In her mind, she had been justified. Her husbands, her son—they were all hers. They had no right to leave her, to betray her love. When questioned, she stated calmly, "I gave them peace. They will never leave me now."

Psychologists who examined her during the trial were baffled by her mental state. On the surface, Vera seemed perfectly sane—her speech was measured, her demeanor composed. But beneath that calm exterior lay a mind warped by jealousy and obsession. She couldn't bear the thought of anyone leaving her, and in her twisted logic, killing them was the only way to ensure they remained hers forever.

Vera was sentenced to life in prison, where she remained until her death. She spent the rest of her days in a cold cell, isolated from the world she had once controlled. In the end, she never admitted that what she had done was wrong.

In her mind, she was not a murderer—she was simply a woman who loved too much.

Vera Renczi's story is a haunting one. It serves as a chilling reminder of the dangers of unchecked possessiveness, of the way love can twist into something dark and destructive. Her beauty and charm allowed her to deceive those around her, but beneath that charm lay a heart capable of unimaginable cruelty.

Her legacy is one of fear and fascination. How could someone who seemed so refined, so elegant, commit such horrors? How could a mother kill her own child out of jealousy? Vera's case raised questions that still resonate today, about the nature of obsession, the power of control, and the lengths some will go to keep hold of those they love.

Today, the name Vera Renczi still evokes a shudder, a reminder of the darkness that can lurk behind even the most charming of smiles. She remains one of Romania's most infamous criminals, a woman whose life was defined by her need to possess, to control, to destroy. And though the details of her life and crimes may have faded with time, the lessons her story teaches about love, obsession, and control remain as relevant as ever.

44. The Sordid Story

I n the quiet town of Richford, New York, where the landscape was dotted with rolling hills and the air was often filled with the scent of blooming flowers, Waneta Hoyt seemed to live an ordinary life. She was a wife, a mother, and a familiar face in her small community. People who knew her described her as kind, gentle, and deeply devoted to her family. But behind this calm exterior lay a heart-wrenching story that would leave an indelible mark on the town and shock the nation.

Born on May 13, 1946, Waneta Charnock grew up in Richford, a place where life moved at a slower pace, and neighbors knew each other by name. Her childhood seemed unremarkable—there were no signs of what was to come. Like many young girls in the 1950s, she dreamed of marriage, children, and a simple, happy life. Waneta wasn't one to stand out in school. She was quiet, shy, and kept to herself. There was no indication then that beneath her unassuming demeanor, dark clouds were already forming.

In 1965, at the age of 19, Waneta married Tim Hoyt, a local man she had known for some time. Their life together seemed typical for the era. Tim worked hard to support his family, while Waneta settled into her role as a homemaker, taking care of the house and garden. Their marriage, while not perfect, appeared stable. But as the years went by, it became evident that something was terribly wrong within the Hoyt household.

Waneta and Tim had five children, and each child's arrival was met with joy and hope for a bright future. First came Eric, then Julie, followed by James, Molly, and finally Noah. But tragedy struck, and one by one, their children died, each under mysterious circumstances. Between 1965 and 1971, all five children were gone, their deaths attributed to Sudden Infant Death Syndrome (SIDS), a diagnosis that was not well understood at the time. Doctors, baffled by the recurring deaths, expressed their condolences and moved on, but no one could make sense of the Hoyt family's unimaginable loss.

Waneta mourned publicly, her face etched with sorrow. To neighbors, she was a picture of grief, a mother whose heart had been shattered five times over. "She was so gentle with her children," one neighbor recalled. "I never suspected anything. How could I?" But beneath the surface, something far more sinister was at play.

For years, no one questioned the deaths. SIDS, while rare, was considered a tragic but natural cause of death. Waneta's ability to grieve openly and convincingly masked the horror that was slowly unfolding. It wasn't until much later that medical professionals began to look deeper into the Hoyt children's deaths, questioning how five children from the same family could die under such similar circumstances. This kind of tragedy, happening repeatedly in one family, raised alarms.

As investigators delved into the details of each child's death, the picture began to shift. The initial diagnosis of SIDS no longer seemed to fit. The deaths followed a pattern, a chilling one. All five children had died suddenly while in their mother's care, and each death came shortly after signs of illness that doctors could never fully explain.

The truth unraveled in 1994 when authorities reopened the case. Under intense scrutiny and questioning, Waneta broke down and confessed. She had smothered her children to death. The reasons she gave were heart-wrenching. She claimed that the babies wouldn't stop crying and that they were too much for her to handle. "I just couldn't take it," she said in a chilling confession. Waneta, it seemed, had been overwhelmed by the demands of motherhood. Her deep psychological turmoil, unrecognized by those around her, had festered into an unthinkable crime.

It became clear that Waneta Hoyt suffered from severe postpartum depression, a mental illness that, at the time, was poorly understood and rarely diagnosed. Her feelings of inadequacy, combined with the crushing demands of caring for her children, created a perfect storm. But while postpartum depression is a condition that many mothers experience, Waneta's actions go beyond the despair it causes. She had crossed a line that few could comprehend.

In 1995, Waneta Hoyt was convicted of second-degree murder for the deaths of her children. The courtroom was silent as the verdict was read. Tim Hoyt, her husband, sat in the back, staring blankly at the proceedings. He, too, had been a victim in many ways—unaware of the horror that had taken place in his own home. The case sent shockwaves through the country, not just because of the nature of the crime, but because of what it revealed about maternal mental health and the hidden struggles that can exist within families.

"She was the last person I would have suspected," a neighbor said after the trial. "We all felt sorry for her. I never imagined..." That was the sentiment echoed by many who had known Waneta. She had seemed so normal, so loving. But as the trial revealed, even those closest to her could not see the torment she carried inside.

Psychologists who evaluated Waneta spoke of her deep-seated feelings of helplessness and inadequacy. They described her as someone who had felt trapped by the responsibilities of motherhood, a woman whose mental health had deteriorated to the point where she believed the only solution was to stop the crying, to end the lives of her children. But even these explanations felt hollow to the families of the victims. How could a mother kill her own children?

The case raised uncomfortable questions about the nature of maternal instincts. Society often assumes that mothers are naturally nurturing, protective figures. But Waneta Hoyt's story shattered that assumption. It forced people to confront the reality that motherhood, for some, is not a source of joy but of overwhelming pressure and despair. It also highlighted the dangers of untreated mental illness and the devastating consequences that can result when those in need of help go unnoticed.

Today, Waneta Hoyt's name is remembered as a chilling reminder of the fragility of the human mind and the darkness that can exist behind closed doors. Her crimes, though committed decades ago, still resonate in discussions about maternal mental health, postpartum depression, and the importance of early intervention. Waneta's story is not just one of tragedy but of the failures of a system that was ill-equipped to recognize the signs of a mother in distress.

Looking back, it is easy to wonder how things might have turned out differently. Could her children have been saved if someone had recognized the signs earlier? Could Waneta have been helped if she had received the support she needed? These are questions that remain unanswered, leaving behind a legacy of grief, confusion, and sorrow.

In the end, Waneta Hoyt's story is one of profound loss—of innocence, of trust, and of life itself. Her children, whose lives were cut tragically short, are remembered as victims of not just their mother's actions, but of a society that failed to protect them. Waneta's tale serves as a stark reminder of the complexities of the human mind and the devastating consequences that can result when those complexities are left unchecked.

Though Waneta Hoyt is long gone, her story lives on as a cautionary tale. It is a reminder that beneath the surface of seemingly ordinary lives, there can sometimes lurk unimaginable darkness.

45. The Haunting Tale

In the gritty, post-war streets of Newcastle upon Tyne, amidst the industrial hum and working-class struggle of the 1960s, a name would soon grip the nation in shock and disbelief—Mary Bell. Her story, twisted with tragedy and violence, shattered the illusion that childhood was synonymous with innocence. She became notorious as one of Britain's youngest killers, her actions casting a long shadow over juvenile crime and the dark potential of neglected youth.

Mary Flora Bell was born on May 26, 1957, into a world already marked by hardship. She came to life in the run-down Scotswood area, where poverty clung to families and opportunities seemed like distant dreams. Her mother, Betty Bell, was young, troubled, and deeply unfit for motherhood. She struggled with mental health issues and worked as a prostitute, leaving her daughter alone for long periods. There was no father figure in Mary's life, just a string of men who came and went, offering little stability. The neglect Mary suffered in those early years left an imprint—a wound that would later manifest in the most disturbing ways.

As a child, Mary was a quiet girl, yet there was something about her that set her apart. Teachers and neighbors described her as withdrawn, troubled, and often difficult. Her childhood was devoid of the warmth and protection that every child needs to thrive. Instead, she learned early on how to fend for herself in a world that offered no safety net. The streets of Scotswood became her playground, and it was there that her darker impulses began to surface.

Though she attended school, Mary found little solace in her education. Her grades were poor, and she struggled to connect with her classmates. She was prone to attention-seeking behavior—acts of defiance that further alienated her from others. Despite her difficulties, there were glimmers of intelligence and creativity in Mary. She loved drawing and writing stories, but these activities were often marred by her increasingly violent tendencies. Her teachers grew concerned as she exhibited troubling behaviors, though no one knew how deep the issues ran.

Mary's home life was a nightmare. Betty Bell, her mother, was emotionally unstable and abusive. Reports later surfaced suggesting that Betty had attempted to harm or even kill Mary on multiple occasions when she was a baby. These acts of cruelty, combined with her mother's neglect, left deep emotional scars. Mary was essentially abandoned by the one person who should have protected her, and in her young mind, she began to internalize the idea that life was cruel and disposable.

By the time Mary was ten years old, the damage had been done. She had befriended another troubled girl, Norma Bell (no relation), and together they roamed the streets unsupervised. While Norma was more of a follower, Mary took the lead in their troubling adventures. It wasn't long before their mischief escalated into something far more sinister.

On May 25, 1968, a day before her eleventh birthday, Mary Bell committed her first murder. The victim was four-year-old Martin Brown, a young boy from the neighborhood. Mary lured Martin into an abandoned house, and there, in cold blood, she strangled him. The death initially baffled authorities. At the time, it was classified as an accident, as there was no obvious sign of foul play. But Mary wasn't done.

In July of the same year, Mary struck again. This time, her victim was three-year-old Brian Howe. Mary, with Norma Bell in tow, led Brian to a remote area and strangled him with her bare hands. But the horror didn't stop there. In a chilling display of cold-hearted cruelty, Mary mutilated the young boy's body with scissors, carving marks into his skin and cutting off clumps of his hair. This second murder sent shockwaves through the community. The brutality of the crime was shocking, especially when the police began to suspect that a child was responsible.

The investigation intensified, and soon, the police turned their attention to Mary and Norma. During questioning, Mary displayed a disturbing detachment from the gravity of the situation. She showed no remorse and instead seemed to relish the attention. When asked about the deaths, she gave conflicting statements, which eventually led to her confession. Mary's cold demeanor and lack of empathy left detectives and the public alike in disbelief. How could a child commit such heinous acts?

The trial of Mary Bell was a media sensation. The courtroom buzzed with the horror of what had transpired, and people struggled to comprehend the psychology of a child who had become a killer. During the trial, Mary's defense argued that she had been deeply damaged by her upbringing. Her mother's neglect and abuse, combined with her exposure to violence from an early age, had warped her understanding of right and wrong. Psychological evaluations revealed that Mary exhibited signs of psychopathy and lacked the emotional development necessary to understand the full impact of her actions.

Still, the jury found her guilty of manslaughter due to diminished responsibility. She was sentenced to an indefinite period in a secure facility for young offenders. The nation breathed a sigh of relief, but the questions remained. How had a young girl fallen so far into darkness? What could be done to prevent such tragedies from happening again?

As Mary Bell served her sentence, her story continued to captivate the public. She remained a figure of fascination, a symbol of innocence corrupted and a chilling reminder of the potential for evil that can lurk even within a child. Over the years, as Mary grew into adulthood, she largely stayed out of the public eye. After her release at the age of 23, she was granted anonymity and given a new identity to protect her from the media frenzy that would have undoubtedly followed her.

Today, Mary Bell's name still conjures up images of a lost childhood twisted by violence and neglect. She remains a polarizing figure, a case study in the complexities of juvenile delinquency and the long-lasting effects of childhood trauma. While many view her as a product of her environment—an innocent girl failed by society—others see her as a cold-blooded killer, someone whose actions, no matter her age, cannot be excused.

Mary Bell's story forces society to confront uncomfortable truths about childhood, innocence, and the impact of abuse. It raises difficult questions about how much a person's upbringing can shape their future and to what extent they can be held accountable for actions taken in the fog of trauma.

Though she is no longer the wide-eyed child who once committed unthinkable acts, the legacy of Mary Bell lingers. Her case continues to haunt the streets of Newcastle, where the memory of Martin Brown and Brian Howe serves as a reminder of the darkness that can sometimes lie beneath the surface of even the most innocent faces.

• • • •